JUDITH MILLER'S
COLOR

JUDITH MILLER'S
COLOR

PERIOD AND REGIONAL STYLE FROM AROUND THE WORLD

PHOTOGRAPHY BY TIM CLINCH

CLARKSON POTTER/PUBLISHERS
NEW YORK

Contents

Published by Clarkson Potter/Publishers, 299 Park Avenue, New York, NY 10171. Member of the Crown Publishing Group. Random House, Inc. New York, Toronto, London, Sydney, Auckland, www.randomhouse.com. Originally published in Great Britain in 2000 by Marshall Editions Ltd.

Clarkson N. Potter is a trademark and Potter and colophon are registered trademarks of Random House, Inc.

Printed in Italy

CHIEF CONTRIBUTORS   John Wainwright, Graham Vickers
PHOTOGRAPHER   Tim Clinch
EDITORS   Christine Davis, Charles Phillips
MANAGING EDITOR   Liz Stubbs
DESIGNER   Nigel Soper
MANAGING ART EDITOR   Flora Awolaja
ART DIRECTOR   Dave Goodman
EDITORIAL DIRECTOR   Ellen Dupont
EDITORIAL COORDINATOR   Ros Highstead
LOCATION AND PICTURE RESEARCHER   Jess Walton
EDITORIAL ASSISTANT   Victoria Cookson
PRODUCTION   Nikki Ingram
AMERICANIZER   Maggi McCormick

Library of Congress Cataloging-in-Publication Data is available upon request

Photograph of Judith Miller by Adrian Weinbrecht; self-portrait of Tim Clinch; all other cover photographs by Tim Clinch

ISBN 0-609-60784-7

10 9 8 7 6 5 4 3 2 1
First American Edition

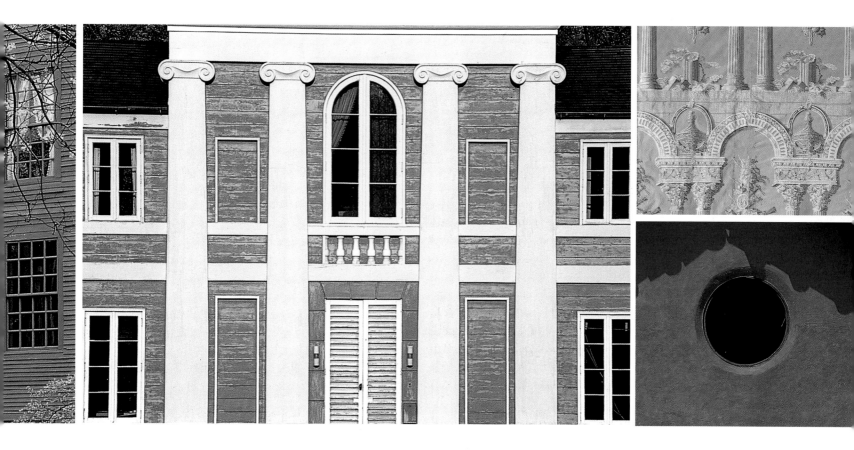

The publishers have made every effort to ensure that the color samples supplied by the manufacturers used throughout this book have been accurately reproduced. However, due to the limitations of the printing process there will be variations in the colors shown.

Foreword

THERE ARE MANY choices to be made when you are decorating and furnishing a home. For example, you will have to decide on fabric and wallpaper patterns, styles of furniture, types of lighting and, if the project is fairly extensive, architectural fixtures and fittings. However, if over 20 years of restoring and redecorating period houses and writing books and presenting television programs on interior decoration has taught me one thing, it is that choosing a color scheme is the most important and potentially rewarding decision you will make. Whether you live in a period or modern home, and whether you wish to decorate in a period or a contemporary style, the purpose of *Color* is to show you the numerous options available and to inspire and guide you to the right choice.

We begin with an overview of the broad trends in the use of color – from the primitive cave paintings of our Paleolithic ancestors, via the domestic and public buildings of ancient Egypt, Greece, and Rome, through the Middle Ages, the Renaissance, and the Georgian and Victorian eras, to our Postmodern world. This is followed by a style section – the heart of the book – which is conveniently broken down into the major historical styles of architecture and decoration fashionable from the early 18th to the early 21st centuries. Each style is further illustrated through a series of individual case studies, which include both authentic period and contemporary recreations or pastiches of the styles.

These are, in turn, augmented with specific palette information which, via color swatches and snapshots of locations, identify the core colors associated with the style and period. For ease of use, each swatch shows a commerically available paint and is keyed to an extensive list of European and American manufacturers given at the back of the book.

In addition to these major historical styles and palettes, we have included a section covering some important national and regional variations – rural Tuscany, postmodern Mexico, contemporary Morocco, and American Shaker – which in recent years have proved increasingly influential beyond their specific geographic locations. You will then find explanations of the aesthetic relationships between different hues, tints, and shades, and the psychological effects of employing the dominant colors: red, yellow, blue, and green. Finally, illustrating the continuity of color in decoration, we show how earth and vegetable pigments first used by our primitive ancestors are still being produced today.

Color has always played a crucial role in complementing the architecture of our immediate surroundings, in personalizing them, and in projecting our sense of fashion and taste. I believe that *Color* will also reveal that, if I may adapt the words of the influential Mexican architect Luis Barragán, it is also the vital ingredient for adding that touch of magic to your home.

JUDITH MILLER, LONDON

CHAPTER 1

A History of Color

ABOVE Straw-yellow walls, gray-blue woodwork and pine floorboards provide the backdrop to Louis XVI furniture at the Château de Montvert, in the Dordogne, France.

LEFT A cement-rendered wall at the Malinalco Golf Club designed by Mexico architect José de Yturbe south of Mexico City, is repainted a distinctive orange-terracotta hue.

FAR LEFT The Neoclassical Sculpture Gallery of the Real Casa del Labrador in Aranjuez, Spain, was designed by Jean-Démosthène Dugourc in the 1790s. The "Trajan's Column" clock in the foreground was added in 1803.

Paleolithic to Contemporary

While factors such as changes of light and variations in the texture of surfaces affect the way in which human eyes and the brain perceive and process the appearance of particular hues, color has always been a potent element in our understanding of the natural world. Just as significantly, we humans have consistently exploited the qualities of color when shaping the world to meet our needs. The desire to embellish our homes with color and pattern and to create an immediate environment that both stimulates and projects our sense of taste and style appears to be a basic instinct that can be traced back to the cave paintings of our most distant ancestors.

Thus it was color as much as line that Paleolithic man used when, having become a conscious participant in life, he first chose to commentate on it by creating two-dimensional art. Some of these early cave paintings survive to the present day. For example, the 15,000-year-old murals discovered in 1940 at the Grotte de Lascaux, in Dordogne, France, display narrative scenes of animals and symbols that seem to mix observation with mythical invention. Rendered in yellow and reddish-brown earth pigments and black derived from carbon, they reveal a basic, easily accessible palette that closely reflects the contemporary surroundings of earth, rock, fur, and blood.

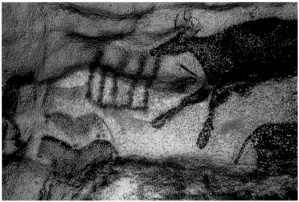

ABOVE This cave painting of a stag and a horse from the Paleolithic period, 15,000 years before the present, was discovered in the Grotte de Lascaux, near Montignac, France. The anonymous artist would have used a basic palette of earth pigments – in this case, predominantly yellow and brown ochers – and black derived from manganese or carbon. The medium in which they were mixed was probably animal fat.

The stylized imagery and limited palette in humans' earliest recorded wall decorations were also to become the defining characteristic of the formalized narrative tomb paintings of ancient Egypt, dating from *c.*3000B.C. While the hieroglyphs and the flat human profiles defined the graphic aspect of ancient Egyptian murals for three millennia, color provided the flavor and much of the symbolism. Men's skin is almost invariably depicted in red ocher, and women's in yellow ocher; similarly, the landscape of the Nile Valley is repeatedly reduced to simple chromatic elements: red/yellow desert, green papyrus, blue river, and bleached blue sky.

"The essence of Egyptian colour usage is three-to-four colour combinations hinged on red or yellow."

(Margaret Walch and Augustine Hope, colorists)

In addition to the basic red, yellow and brown earth colors, white obtained from gypsum and black from soot, the pigments employed by the ancient Egyptians included strong yellow from orpiment (a sulfide of arsenic); blue from lapis lazuli or a high-temperature fusion of silica, copper, and powdered calcium; and green from malachite and chrysocolla, or a mixture of the aforementioned yellow and blue pigments – a combination that gave the resulting green a distinctive blue cast. Suspended in water-soluble gum to create tempera paints and applied as thin washes within red ocher outline drawings on plaster, these pigments dried flat and usually opaque – qualities, like the addition of black key lines to make figures stand out, that were typical of ancient Egyptian decoration.

ABOVE Paintings from the tomb of Sennufer, one of the Tombs of the Nobles at Thebes, depict the daily life of the ancient Egyptians. They are rendered in red and yellow ochers, orpiment (a yellow sulfide of arsenic), white (from gypsum), and black (from soot) – all on a plaster ground covered with a thin yellow colorwash. Two other favored ground colors in Pharaonic tomb painting were white and bluish gray. The strong colors have faded since the tombs were opened up in the early 20th century.

For many centuries, it was commonly believed that the ancient Greeks favored white as a decorative finish – a misconception based on observations of the bleached white temple ruins of Greek antiquity that were eventually disproved by mid-18th-century archeological excavations of original Greek interiors.

ABOVE The highly stylized ancient Greek "Toreador Fresco" from the Knossos Palace on Crete combines a range of rich earth tones – derived from iron- and manganese-rich clays – with white and black on a contrasting bright blue and turquoise ground.

In fact, many Greek buildings were polychromatic and decorated with a palette of pigments similar to that of ancient Egypt, but with a number of additions – most notably, lead-based red and white. Black, and harmonious buff, tobaccolike orange-brown terracotta and red hues derived from iron- and manganese-rich clays were particularly prevalent, but saturated and vibrant yellow, blue, green, and gold were also much in evidence – not only as solid wall colors and in narrative murals, but also as a means of highlighting sculptural architectural forms and details.

The early Roman palette differed from the ancient Greek in featuring subtle shades of yellow, green, mauve, and blue-gray, although the Greeks' love of rich, saturated color was echoed in later Roman decoration – as at Pompeii in Italy. Excavations there have revealed rooms painted deep red from floor to ceiling and sophisticated murals in which extensive use is made of architectural and narrative *trompe l'oeil* techniques, and *faux marbre* finishes. The colors – mainly earth and mineral pigments mixed with beeswax and resin – were given additional resonance by burnishing with marble rollers and cloths.

ABOVE This detail of a Roman interior near Pompeii, dating from the first century A.D., reveals highly sophisticated painted decoration dominated by *trompe l'oeil* and *faux marbre* effects. The use of strong, rich colors – notably red, dark brown, and purplish black, derived from earth and mineral pigments – is also characteristic of Roman decoration in grander houses of the period.

LEFT Built between 1392 and *c.*1407, the gothic chateau Pierrefonds was restored in the mid-19th century by the influential French architect Viollet-le-Duc (1814–79). The richness of the decorative palette – vibrant blue, saturated green, earthy red, and gold – is matched in this hall by the elaboration of the decorative motifs, which are derived from the romanesque, gothic, and heraldic vocabularies of ornament.

During the Middle Ages – the long period of European feudal history that began with the fall of the Western Roman Empire in the 5th century A.D. and endured until the flowering of the Renaissance in the 14th century – the "secrets" of pigment production came under the control of guilds of colorists, who offered strictly supervised apprenticeships in the grinding and mixing of colors to be used by painter-stainers and fabric dyers. Partly as a consequence of this and partly as a spin-off from technical advances made in the field of fine art, the use of color in decoration became increasingly sophisticated. Moreover, it was expressed – in the churches, palaces, castles, and manor houses of the wealthy ruling classes – through a rich and diverse vocabulary of ornament. The three major strands of ornament were romanesque, which combined classical Roman, oriental, pagan, and Christian forms and motifs; Gothic, which introduced architectural elements such as lancets, foils, and tracery, and a decorative focus on human figures and flora and fauna; and heraldic, which emphasized concepts of chivalry and lineage, manifested in emblems and allegories such as cyphers, coats-of-arms, and the "Tree of Life."

Color and pattern were often applied directly to the stone, plaster, tiled, and wooden surfaces of the principal rooms of wealthy medieval interiors, but they were most evident in the deployment of fabric furnishings such as bed hangings, cushions, imported oriental carpets, and wall-hung tapestries. The use of vegetable and mineral dyes in the tapestries, especially during the late Middle Ages, was particularly sophisticated. Core colors included madder red, woad blue and yellow, and brown from weld. Together with silver and gilt thread, additional colors, created by mixing dyes – and/or using different mordants, such as aluminum and zinc, to set them – included ruby and purple-red, clove pink, blackish blue, and green from weld, woad, and copper.

ABOVE This recreation of a grand late-medieval bedroom is at Leeds Castle in Kent, England. In less affluent dwellings of the period, the walls would have been simply whitewashed, but here they are hung with luxurious, monogrammed silk hangings – a fabric also employed in orange-red for the bedhangings. As in many castles, palaces, and churches of the period, the floor is laid with lead-glazed tiles made from local reddish-brown clay and configured in a checked pattern.

The Renaissance – the grand revival and development of the arts and sciences that emerged in Europe in the 12th century and flourished from the 14th to the 16th centuries – was primarily inspired by Greek and, especially, Roman precedents. In practice, it gave rise to so many variations of style in painting, architecture, and decoration that it cannot be considered a single stylistic movement. However, some aesthetic principles proved common to all variants – most notably the supreme value of harmony and proportion. The decorator's palette – now expanded to include many new hues, tints, and shades, most of mineral origin – was applied with this principle in mind. Various color schemes were fashionable including soft and light, dark and brooding, vibrant and saturated.

LEFT The Villa Barbaro, in Masera, Italy, was designed by the highly influential Italian architect Andrea Palladio and was constructed 1550–60. Inspired by Classical Roman models, this room is a tour de force of late-Renaissance architecture, ornament and decoration. The natural stone colors of the architectural fixtures are complemented by the soft greens, reds, and yellows employed by Venetian painter Paolo Veronese in his magnificent *trompe l'oeil* frescoes.

Some of the most significant color schemes were to be found in the residential work of the Italian architect Andrea Palladio (1508–80). The architectural harmonies of his villas were complemented by a palette of cool, elegant whites and a range of subtle pastel hues deployed in sophisticated murals of classical imagery. Although superseded in the 17th century by the flamboyant baroque style, with its grandiose ornamentation, and in Louis XIV's France by a sumptuous shimmering palette of gilt, crystal, and rich brown, green, and red, Palladio's more restrained and elegant style was to enjoy, at least in principle, a notable revival in the early 18th century.

ABOVE The Galerie des Glaces ("Hall of Mirrors") at the Palace of Versailles was designed by French architects Charles Le Brun and Jules Hardouin-Mansart. A highly reflective corridor of mirror-glass, crystal, gilt, and variegated marbles, it encapsulates the overtly Classical variant of the baroque style that was fashionable in France during the reign of Louis XIV (1643–1715).

LEFT Chiswick House in London was built in the 1720s for the 3rd Earl of Burlington. As elsewhere in the house, the architectural features of the Red Room are inspired by classical Roman and late-renaissance prototypes and display the harmony of proportion and detail characteristic of early 18th-century Palladianism. The combination of rich red wall hangings and yellow damask upholstery, color-coordinated with the gilded architectural moldings, illustrates Palladian decoration at its grandest.

The 18th-century reaction to what many considered the architectural and decorative excesses of the baroque style manifested itself in a number of ways. In early Georgian England (see pp.30–35), architects such as Colen Campbell (1673–1729) and William Kent (1685–1748) drew on the Palladian model for inspiration, although in the grandest neo-Palladian interiors, their decorative palette was generally richer and more saturated than that of the prototype – with stronger, more vibrant colors evident in hangings and upholstery.

As with many styles of architecture and decoration fashionable during other historical periods, the neo-Palladian

"Palladianism emerged in part as a reaction to what the influential Scottish architect Colen Campbell described as the 'affected and licentious' ornamentation of the Baroque style."

(John Wainwright, author)

style was, for reasons of cost, diluted in more ordinary houses. In general, it took the form of fewer and plainer architectural fixtures and fittings, as well as more rudimentary and sparser furnishings. In particular, it manifested itself in much greater use of softwood wall paneling, instead of expensive paper or fabric wall hangings. The paneling, sometimes grained in imitation of finely figured hardwoods, was more usually colored with oil paints – favored hues included a range of "stone" colors, "drabs" (muddy brown and green), and by the middle of the 18th century, brighter hues such as shell pink and pea green.

Painted wood also featured very prominently on the western side of the Atlantic, where the increasingly prosperous American colonies began to turn from a utilitarian pioneer existence to the "luxuries" of architecture and interior decoration (see pp.36–53). Mostly via trade and imported pattern books, the early Georgian neo-Palladian model provided the blueprint, but was adapted to local conditions in the Colonial style. The abundance of forests meant that the great majority of colonial houses were wood-framed, weatherboarded, and internally paneled. These wooden surfaces were colored – initially with milk- or oil-based paints tinted with indigenous earth pigments, but as the 18th century wore on also with more expensive imported pigments – and were a key component of Colonial style.

ABOVE The dining room of the George Wythe House, which was built in Williamsburg, Virginia, in the 1750s, is decorated and furnished in the rather austere, masculine style favored for such rooms in American colonial houses during the mid-18th century. The palette for the plastered walls and ceilings, and the woodwork, is restricted to white and grayish green – a popular combination.

Back in continental Europe, reaction to the baroque emerged in the form of the rococo style (see pp.54–9). Originating in France and gradually disseminated throughout most of mainland Europe (and also Sweden), rococo decoration was characterized by assymetrical, curvaceous forms – such as shell motifs, scrollwork, and undulating foliage – and *chinoiserie* imagery. Generally, these delicate, sinuous forms were enhanced by a palette of gold, white, and ivory, and pastel blue, green, pink, and yellow – although, in countries such as Portugal, richer, stronger colors were often employed.

By the mid-18th century, as part of what can be seen as an historical continuum of action and reaction, rococo came to be judged as rather frivolous and was gradually supplanted by the more serious neoclassical style. Inspired by excavations of classical Greek and Roman sites, notably at Pompeii and Herculaneum in Italy, neoclassicism took root on both sides of the Atlantic and, just as the Renaissance had done, gave rise to numerous "sub-styles" (see pp.60–115). Although often modified by other vocabularies of ornament – such as Egyptian, oriental, and "Gothick" in the English Regency – these styles were united by two strands, an emphasis on the architectural symmetry and proportion of classical architecture and an increasingly sophisticated and varied use of color.

LEFT Designed in the 1740s by G.W. von Knobelsdorff (1699–1753), Sans Souci Palace at Potsdam, Germany, typifies the grander and more stately Teutonic variant of the originally light and frivolous French Rococo style. In this room, a bright and lustrous yellow lacquer paint on the wall paneling is picked up to match the yellow *portières* and upholstery and provides the backdrop for a profusion of painted rococo imagery. Prominent among this are sprigs and garlands of flowers, exotic birds, and *chinoiserie* figures.

BELOW The library at Kenwood House in London, England, is one of Robert Adam's finest and most elegant interiors. The symmetry and proportion evident in the deployment of architectural forms and decorative motifs derived from the classical vocabulary of ornament is further defined by a palette of gold and white, blue and pink – the two last of almost equal tonal value, and all typical Adam colors that were popular in the late 18th century.

ABOVE Sir John Soane's house in London, England, was constructed 1792–1824. The decorations and furnishings are primarily inspired by classical prototypes, and the rich colors evident in the paint finishes and fabrics not only represent the early 19th-century English palette at its grandest, but also herald the richer, darker colors that became fashionable in mid-Victorian interiors. The walls around this cantilevered, open-string staircase are finished with panels of sienna *faux marbre* – above a wall string of black-and-gold *faux marbre*. The red and gold flame-and-leaf pattern stair carpet is anchored with brass rods.

Underpinning this was a new understanding of the principles of how different hues, tints, and shades related to one another and of how humans responded to them. One of the most influential publications in this field was Moses Harris's *The Natural History of Colours* (1766). As a consequence, influential architects and decorators, such as Robert Adam (1728–92), John Nash (1752–1835), and Sir John Soane (1753–1837) in England, and Charles Percier (1764–1838) and Pierre Fontaine (1762–1835) in France, were better able to exploit qualities such as chromatic intensity and the tonal relationships between different hues, tints, and shades, to enhance not only the overall composition of architectural fixtures and fittings, but also to adjust the perception of light and space within different rooms.

Many styles of architecture and decoration, mainly inspired by classical, gothic and oriental prototypes and often highly eclectic, became fashionable at different periods during the Victorian era (see pp.116–129). In terms of color, the most significant development was the mid-19th century invention of aniline dyes synthesized from coal tar. Initially used in fabrics, then wallpapers, and finally paints, these intense, vivid hues gave rise to a series of rich "High Victorian" color schemes that, inevitably, gave rise to a counter-reaction.

LEFT The Royal Pavilion in Brighton, England, was designed 1786–7 for the Prince Regent (later King George IV) by Henry Holland and extensively remodeled in 1815–22 by John Nash. In the Banqueting Hall, Greek, Roman, Egyptian, and oriental forms and motifs are rendered in a combination of crystal, gilt, polished hardwood and sumptuous colors such as Etruscan red.

The move away from the rich color schemes, stylistic eclecticism, cluttered furnishings, and extravagant use of fabrics characteristic of High Victorian interiors began with the Arts and Crafts and Aesthetic movements during the late 19th century. The lighter Aesthetic palette included colors such as ivory, pale gray, and an olive green known as "greenery-yallery" that, together with more muted hues such as burgundy, "old rose," and hyacinth blue, also proved popular in Arts and Crafts interiors.

ABOVE A circular plan, semi-opaque vacuum-glass brick walls, plate-glass steel-frame doors, a white ceiling, and a black stone (marble) floor give this Modernist dining room an industrial feel. The house, designed in 1931 by Edward Durrell Stone, is in Westchester County, New York.

However, the reaction to High Victorian style was really consolidated under the aegis of the Modern movement (see pp.130–5) during the early 20th century. Indeed, industrialist Henry Ford's celebrated dictum for the motor car – "any color as long as it's black" – could have been adapted by the Modernists simply by substituting the word "white." For example, as early as 1904 the renowned English decorators Cowtan & Sons commented: "We seem to have done everything flatted white or enamelled white paint." In the late 1920s, Mrs. Syrie Maugham created her influential "All White Room" at her London home, while Elsie de Wolfe (1865–1950) designed very similar interiors in the United States.

Underpinning this extensive use of white was the Modernists' response to the rationality of the machine age – namely, to strip buildings of what were seen as superfluous trimmings and to make form the object of aesthetic admiration. Form would be

"Styles of (Modernist) interior furnishing were developed according to the same purist, rationalist tenets as the architecture."

(Phillipa Lewis and Gillian Darley, authors)

LEFT Mies van der Rohe (1886–1969) designed the German Pavilion for the International Exposition in Barcelona, Spain (1928–9). A paradigm for the Modern movement, it incorporated chromium-plate-clad steel columns to support a flat roof and featured walls of onyx and marble slab, some of which penetrated the roof. Colors are characteristically restricted to those intrinsic to the materials.

determined by function, and function depended no more upon the most fashionable color than it did upon curlicues, finials, decorative friezes and other "superfluous" architectural fixtures and fittings. In other words, "less is more."

In actual fact, white did not dominate exclusively as an applied color in the Modernist world. Decorators were happy to give surfaces an inflection of a hue as long as the pigment did not disguise, divert, or detract from form and they made use of various off-whites and pale stone colors. Equally, the inherent colors of natural materials – such as those of wood and variegated stones such as marble – were acceptable. Ultimately, natural light mediated by glass was at the heart of many Modernist homes and, together with concrete and steel, was used in pursuit of the fashionable idea of "a machine for living in" by obliquely evoking the lines of ships, trains, or airplanes – the new icons of the fast-moving industrial age. The effects were frequently subtle and depended upon the suggestive qualities of shape and materials, rather than anything so literal as the colors of the original model. Indeed, the Modernist palette, if it can be so called, was essentially one of industrial finishes rather than pigments.

A rigid doctrine, conceived in Europe by a small group of intellectuals – some of whom later found fame as architects and designers in the United States – Modernism gave rise to some elegantly reductive buildings. However, their example sadly inspired many lesser 20th-century talents in whose work the omission of color was matched by an absence of vision. Again, inevitably, a reaction ensued.

First coined in the 1970s, the term postmodernism (see pp.136–157) has in some respects proved a rather elusive label. Ultimately, it embraces a loss of faith in the stripped-down, colorless ideology of Modernism and an acknowledgement that the contemporary world is visually and culturally more diverse than at any previous time in history. Fifteen thousand years after the cave painters worked with simple colors in a medium with no past, we can now call upon a vast array of natural and synthetic pigments and paints (notably synthetic, water-based latex-emulsions), as well as optically generated color and countless sophisticated decorative techniques. We also have access to thousands of years of architectural and decorative styles – an historical gallery of the past that has inevitably conditioned our contemporary visual attitudes.

"The second half of the 20th century witnessed a rejection of Modernism's unremitting rationality and minimal use of colour and pattern."

(John Wainwright, author)

ABOVE As part of the reaction to the effects of Modernism on Mexican architecture, there was a full-blooded return to the use of color. Traditional indigenous hues, first employed in pre-Colonial Mesoamerican civilizations were pressed into service in Post-Modernism to create luminous spaces and dynamic juxtapositions of color and tone.

All this information, put into practise, has given rise to a wide and diverse range of contemporary styles. On one hand, the architectural fixtures and fittings, and the color schemes originally employed in surviving period houses – dating from the Middle Ages onward – have often been lovingly and authentically restored. On the other hand, as part of a process in which the past is reappraised through the eyes of the present, earlier styles of architecture, ornament, and decoration have been revived and reinterpreted to meet contemporary needs. This latter phenomenon has been especially marked in Mexico, where postmodern architects and designers have found new inspiration in pre-Colonial Mesoamerican forms, motifs, and colors. There has also been a new appreciation of national and regional differences – of styles and palettes previously outside the historical mainstream, such as those of rural Tuscany, Morocco, and the American Shakers.

Postmodern color schemes and decorative styles have proved particularly versatile. Used not only to recreate or reinvent the past, but also to evoke – unlike the primitive cave paintings of our earliest ancestors – numerous cultures and locations far beyond our own immediate surroundings, the postmodern palette is almost without limitations.

2

Major Historical Palettes

ABOVE The Richard Mandel House, Bedford Hills, New York, was built in the 1930s in the Modernist style. The chair and table in the open-plan living area are by Donald Deskey.

LEFT The Blue Room of the Villa di Geggiano, near Siena in Italy, retains its original hand-finished *trompe l'oeil* wallpaper which, like the painted furniture, dates to the 1770s.

FAR LEFT This grand salon in a 17th-century French chateau was restored by Andrew Allfree. The painted *faux marbre* fireplace dates to 1700, the *boiseries* to the early 18th century.

Early Georgian style

LEFT This ground-floor kitchen-breakfast room in an early 18th-century London townhouse displays in its architectural fixtures and fittings the fundamental symmetry of proportion that typifies early Georgian style. The combination of yellowish off-whites, reddish brown, and yellowish brown serves to consolidate the effect.

ABOVE Six-over-six sliding sash windows were commonly installed in early Georgian houses. Their frames and glazing bars, like the softwood wall paneling in this living room, are painted a semigloss yellow.

T HE PREDOMINANT STYLE of architecture in England during the reigns of George I (1714–27) and George II (1727–60) was Palladianism. Emerging as a reaction to what many considered to be the unwarranted complexities of the 17th-century baroque style, this restrained form of Classicism was primarily inspired by the buildings, writings, and engravings of the 16th-century Italian architect Andrea Palladio – most notably, the first English translation (in 1715) of his *Quattro Libri dell'Architettura* (1570). Founded on Roman (rather than Greek) and renaissance prototypes and promoted by architects such as Colen Campbell and William Kent, and influential patrons of the arts such as the 3rd Earl of Burlington, Palladian architecture at its grandest was characterized by large temple-front porticos, rusticated masonry, vaulted ceilings, and tripartite Venetian windows. It was further augmented by richly colored fabric and paper hangings, together with gilded architectural moldings and furniture with seating often upholstered to match the color and pattern of the window treatment or wall finish.

When translated into smaller, less affluent houses, this early Georgian style of architecture and decoration – which also became very fashionable in the American colonies (see pp.36–53) – took on a more modest guise. Ceilings were mostly flat-plastered rather than vaulted and embellished with moldings; painted softwood wall paneling was used instead of expensive silk or paper wall hangings; far less use was made of gilding on moldings and furniture; and the distribution of solid, well-crafted Georgian furniture was generally relatively sparse. Yet the key elements of the style were not compromised: in terms of architectural fixtures and fittings, furnishings, and the use of color, the emphasis remained firmly on harmony of proportion and detail and, above all, on domestic comfort.

ABOVE Full-height softwood wall paneling, woodgrained or, as here, flat-painted, provided good insulation and a cheaper alternative to silk hangings or handprinted papers in ordinary early Georgian houses.

LEFT The exteriors of early Georgian brick townhouses were largely unornamented; the symmetry of the simple architectural components was echoed, as here, in the full-height wall paneling within. Made of pine or fir, this paneling is painted in one of the flat, gray "stone" colors – not dissimilar to the hue of the brickwork opposite – popular during the first half of the 18th century.

ABOVE Blue was a highly fashionable color in early Georgian interiors. While lighter sky blues were sometimes used, darker, richer shades were more common. Such blues also often appeared in silk wall hangings and wallpapers.

RIGHT In what is now the study of the Spitalfields townhouse, the softwood wall paneling and window shutters have been flat-painted in dark grayish green and deep shell-pink. The color contrast helps to define the simple rectilinear configuration of the wooden moldings and provides a tonally sympathetic backdrop for the display of early 18th-century ebonized and gilt-framed paintings and engravings.

BELOW When used, expensive paper or fabric wall hangings were confined to the principal receiving rooms of early Georgian houses. Here a two-tone, muted yellow paper has been hung, its colors closely matching those of the ceiling, chimneypiece, and upholstery. Also characteristic of such rooms are the swagged, tailed, and tasseled valances and the Oriental rug floorcovering.

A SPITALFIELDS TOWNHOUSE

THIS DOUBLE-FRONTED early Georgian townhouse is located in the Spitalfields district of east London, and was constructed in the 1720s – a period of substantial demand for new accommodation from the city's rapidly expanding merchant classes. The housebuilder was Marmaduke Smith, a master-carpenter who lived there from 1726 to 1738; for the rest of the 18th century, it was occupied by Peter Campart, a Huguenot weaver.

Since the late 17th century, Spitalfields had absorbed a large influx of Huguenots fleeing France to escape persecution after the revocation in 1685 of the 1598 Edict of Nantes, which had guaranteed their religious and civil liberties for the best part of a century. Mostly weavers,

notably of fine silk damasks and brocades, and increasingly affluent from supplying the wealthy homeowners of early Georgian England (and the American colonies) with luxury fabrics for upholstery, drapes, and wall hangings, they would have resided on the middle floors of such houses, worked their looms in the well-lit attic rooms, and used parts of the ground floors as retail outlets.

By the 1850s, the house had fallen into disrepair and, in the early 20th century, it was used as a banana warehouse and for lodgings. Acquired by the Spitalfields Historic Buildings Trust in 1977, it was sold in 1979 to the now-deceased art dealer and advisor on historic churches, Michael Gillingham, who, together with his friend Donald

Findlay and the architect Julian Harrap, painstakingly restored the property. Fortunately, the house had retained most of its original architectural fixtures and fittings including a magnificent mahogany staircase, six-over-six sliding sash windows, butt-jointed pine flooring, various marble chimneypieces, and the original Georgian doors, window shutters, and full-height wall paneling.

The architectural integrity of the house's interior was consolidated by its redecoration – particularly with flat and semi-gloss, slightly muted off-white, gray, yellow, green, and pink, which were typical of the early Georgian palette. Together with period fabrics and wallpapers, these paint colors provide the appropriate backdrop for pieces of fine Georgian furniture, as well as displays of paintings, engravings, and artifacts typical of a well-appointed early 18th-century London townhouse.

THIS PAGE Two flat-painted tones of green and a pinkish-stone color have been used on softwood wall paneling in a converted bathroom (above) and a living room (above left) of the Spitalfields townhouse. The yellow and white tones used on the paneling on the stairs (left) provide a stronger contrast.

Using the early Georgian palette

Off-white, gray, and other "stone" colors were often employed for plastered and softwood-paneled walls in the Georgian interiors of the first half of the 18th century; darker, more muted tones included "drabs" (these included muddy browns or greens). Alternatively, much more vibrant saturated colors, such as pea green, sky and royal blue, candy pink, and yellow ocher were also favored. However, the instability of some period pigments and paints made them susceptible to rapid fading and, sometimes, streaking. Colored fabrics also played a significant role: rich green, blue, and gold silks and velvets were much in evidence, as were shell-pinks, crimsons, deep violets, pale lavenders, indigo blues, lemon yellows, and sage greens prevalent in printed calico imported from Calicut on the southwestern coast of India.

RIGHT Green was an extremely fashionable color for painting softwood wall paneling in the Georgian interiors of the first half of the 18th century. The subtle mottling that is evident in this modern finish is caused by the exposure to light of the fugitive pigments in the paint.

BELOW The rusty brown and apricot pink used on the walls are muted in an early Georgian style. The slightly yellowish white on the window frames and flat-plastered ceiling provides a contrast that serves to define the simple symmetry of architecture and moldings.

ABOVE Stone colors including gray were fashionable finishes for wall paneling. The regimented display of gilt-framed pictures is also characteristic of the early to mid-Georgian period.

LEFT The dark shade of straw yellow that has been applied to the elegant sash window frame and surround combines effectively with the off-white coloring on the ceiling to create a warm and invigorating interior.

ABOVE Various off-white colors were mixed by Georgian decorators by adding small amounts of black or blue to white for cooler colors, or yellow or red for a warmer tint.

ABOVE RIGHT A matte brownish-stone color on the wall paneling and room door is contrasted with a deep yellow on the frame and doors of a built-in closet.

RIGHT Upholstery and hangings were sometimes used as a source of color in early Georgian interiors. Favored plain and patterned fabrics included damask and velvet made from silk, wool, linen and, as on this row of spools, cotton.

RIGHT & FAR RIGHT Softwood paneling, sometimes grained in imitation of more expensive finely figured hardwoods, was more often painted, usually a single color or, like the two-tone green paneling (far right), with different shades of the same hue highlighting the moldings. This effect can also be accentuated by using stronger contrasts of color as with the shell-pink center panels and gray-green stiles and rails of the shutters (right).

DULUX COLOUR SELECTOR
Sunburst

DULUX COLOUR SELECTOR
Hot Ginger

BRATS LTD
MEDITERRANEAN PALETTE
Messina · 156

RALPH LAUREN PAINTS
SANTA FE COLLECTION
Albuquerque · SF04A

J.W. BOLLOM & CO. LTD
NATURAL COLOR SYSTEM
S 2040–R8OB

PAINT MAGIC/
JOCASTA INNES
Jade

THE CASA PAINT CO.
Olivine

ACE ILLUMINATIONS
Flint · 178–C

MARSTON & LANGINGER
Taupe

American Colonial style

LEFT This open-string staircase at the Silas Deane House, which was built in 1766 in Wethersfield, Connecticut, has elaborately turned mahogany balusters and newel post. Stained and polished hardwoods such as mahogany were much more expensive than painted softwoods like pine or fir, and their use was a reflection of the affluence of the household. The combination of the grayish-green painted wall paneling and whitewashed plaster seen here is typical of American Colonial decoration of the period.

THE COLONIAL HERITAGE of the United States reflects a more complex and diverse development of style than is sometimes supposed. Often thought of as a single stylistic "look," American Colonial architecture and decoration has its roots in the tastes of the continent's European and Scandinavian immigrants, all of whom brought with them something of the building customs and decorative palettes of their respective mother countries. These were inevitably modified by the kind of materials available locally (notably, an abundance of wood) and by climatic conditions in specific parts of the new country. Accordingly, several distinct styles developed, all of which can be labeled "colonial." For example, the territories of the American Southwest, being under Spanish influence, were introduced to elements of the European Renaissance and Baroque. It was New England, however, that was to become the principal focus of what is most commonly referred to as Colonial style.

The precursor of that style was medieval in origin and was essentially a reinvention of the vernacular wood-framed houses and barns of England and continental northern Europe. With relatively little modification, such buildings proved suitable for the harsh conditions that had greeted the first settlers. Oak frames and clapboard sidings, wattle-and-daub insulation, and whitewashed interiors were the norm, with ornamentation and color playing only a minor role in what were simply unashamed expressions of functional and structural needs. By the early 18th century, however, colonial builders began to build houses in a new spirit of self-confidence. They began to employ more sophisticated architectural forms, together with ornament and color, as emblems of the gradual transition from pioneer subsistence to civic sophistication – from societies founded on religious hope to societies built on self-reliance and ever-increasing commercial success.

ABOVE From the late 17th century, most Colonial houses had Georgian-style paneled doors. This example, at the Isaac Stevens House in Wethersfield, is picked out in blue within a blue-black frame of simple moldings, surrounded by cream clapboard sidings. The door is divided so the upper half can be left open in summer.

ABOVE Like that of the Isaac Stevens House (see left), the front door of the Silas Deane House, also in Wethersfield, is contrasted with its surround: here, a dark iron-oxide red is set against white. The configuration of the door paneling is more elaborate, however, indicating the wealth of the occupants. The Classical frame is equally sophisticated.

LEFT The clapboard facade of the Silas Deane House has been repainted a grayish-blue hue to match the original color of the house (recently identified by scientific paint analysis). The door frame and "twelve-over-twelve" sliding sash windows are picked out in white against the clapboard. The use of contrasting color for architectural fixtures and fittings helps to define these features within the facade and accentuates the symmetry and proportion characteristic of Colonial Georgian architecture.

ABOVE The Webb House in Wethersfield, built in 1752, also has a clapboard facade, which has been repainted to match the original iron-oxide red. Unlike the Silas Deane and Isaac Stevens houses, however, the windows have not been picked out in contrasting colors. Note the porch, a feature of grander Colonial houses around this time.

LEFT The parlor at the George Wythe House, built in the 1750s in Williamsburg, reflects the rising affluence of the American colonies in the second half of the 18th century. Block-printed or flocked wallpapers often replaced painted or wood-paneled plaster walls in grander houses.

BELOW The blue and white fabric used for the bed hangings, daybed, and window drapes in this bedroom in the Silas Deane house features one of the exotic bird-and-flower patterns inspired by Chinese export porcelain that became particularly fashionable during this period.

BELOW RIGHT The gradual move toward a greater diversity of pattern and color in Colonial houses during the 18th century is illustrated by another bedroom at the Silas Deane House. Green paneling contrasts with the red and white bed hangings and rug.

Architecturally, the "Colonial" style of New England from around 1700 to the Revolution was essentially Georgian (see pp.30–5) – a development substantially fueled by the importation of architectural pattern books from England. Initially, the houses built were of a fairly plain construction, most of them comprising a clapboard-sided rectangular block, with symmetrically positioned windows and topped with pitched roofs and gable ends. However, the material success of those who built and lived in them became gradually more and more evident.

Externally, this expression of affluence often took the form of Classical references such as columned and pedimented porticos, balustrades, and dormers. Inside, painted softwood wall paneling configured with rectilinear Classical-style moldings became fashionable, especially in central halls and rooms. Appreciated for its aesthetic and insulating qualities, the paneling could be taken either to ceiling height (especially on fireplace walls) or to dado level, and in grander households was often embellished with classical pilasters and deep cornices.

The sophistication of these architectural features was mirrored in the furnishings. During the second half of the

LEFT The dining parlor at the Governor's Palace in Williamsburg has been redecorated in accordance with surviving documentary evidence of the original decorations. As befits a room used by a government official, and in contrast to the parlors in ordinary residential buildings, the room is very generously proportioned and incorporates prestigious Classical-style architectural fixtures and fittings. These include a white-vein marble chimneypiece flanked by a pair of pilasters, full-height wooden wall paneling, and a deep dentilled cornice. Equally prestigious is the fine Georgian mahogany furniture, the gilt convex mirror hung above the marble-topped, serpentine-legged serving table, and the diamond-patterned *faux marbre* crumbcloth under the dining table. The cool pale blue and white color scheme is notably less domestic in feel than the warmer palette used in the parlor of the George Wythe House (see opposite left).

18th century, fine-quality Georgian furniture was not only imported from England, but also increasingly made by local craftsmen, notably in Boston. Similarly, richly patterned fabrics and wallpapers were bought in from England and France, but also, toward the end of the century, made in cities such as Philadelphia.

Although European imports continued to play a major role in American architecture and decoration beyond the colonial period into the early years of the United States, the accompanying proliferation of "homemade" products fashioned in North America helped to meet an important demand of the Revolution: namely, the need for an independent decorative and architectural style that owed far less to its former colonial rulers. It was the colonists' use of painted color that did most to fulfill that demand and to distinguish Colonial architecture from its English equivalents. The distinction is most readily evident in the decoration of interior paneling and on the exteriors of Colonial houses with clapboard siding, the latter displaying far greater diversities of color than were possible on brick-built English homes.

As we shall see over the following pages, identification of the authentic Colonial palette has sometimes proved problematical. Errors were made in the course of well-intentioned restorations of Colonial houses – especially in the early 20th century, prior to the introduction of scientific paint analysis that accurately accounts for the effects of light on fugitive pigments. What has never been in doubt, however, is the major role that color played in the development of Colonial style among a people embarking on their experiment in independence.

THE GOVERNOR'S PALACE, WILLIAMSBURG

FROM 1699 UNTIL 1780, when the center of state government was transferred to Richmond, Williamsburg was the political and cultural capital of Virginia. After 1780 it became a quiet college town, and so it remained for some 150 years – until 1926, when a local clergyman persuaded John D. Rockefeller, Jr., to sponsor a project that was to restore or reconstruct some 150 major buildings as they had been in the 18th century. Colonial Williamsburg has subsequently become probably the most important repository of America's Colonial architectural heritage.

After the Wren Building and the Capitol, the Governor's Palace was the third great building of Willliamsburg in the Colonial period. Built between 1706 and 1722, it stood as a symbol for the office of viceroyalty in Britain's largest American colony, and thus it also became the focus of the city's fashionable society – until it burned down in 1781.

The reconstruction of the brick-built, three-story Governor's Palace on its original footings, under the aegis of the Colonial Williamsburg Foundation, began in 1930. From the outset, the rebuilding, redecoration, and refurnishing was fueled by a desire for period authenticity.

In terms of the use of color, the initial redecoration of the rooms was based on the diligent research of the late Susan Higgins Nash, an interior designer who used visual assessment of paint samples in surviving Colonial houses – a technique known as "scrape-and-paint." Her findings were subsequently modified as a result of scientific paint analysis combined with close studies of contemporary inventories, paintings, and engravings. As a result, in the 1990s the rooms were redecorated and furnished to recreate as precisely as possible their appearance during Governor Botetourt's residency in the 18th century.

LEFT Sophisticated decorations, fixtures, and fittings in the ballroom of the Governor's Palace reflect the status of the room. The combination of vibrant blue walls, white-painted dentilled cornice, dado paneling and a Classical door frame (which incorporates pilasters and a broken pediment flanking an armorial crest), all enhanced with gilt highlights, was inspired by grand European models. The expensive Prussian blue pigment used in the wall finish reflects the exclusivity of the room's decorative scheme.

RIGHT A darker blue paint has been applied to the full-height wall paneling, chimneypiece, and cornice in a parlor at the Governor's Palace. Again, expensive Prussian blue pigment was used, probably mixed with white lead, calcium carbonate, and charcoal black. The variegated marble slips, lintel, and hearth of the chimneypiece are another indication of wealth.

LEFT The bedroom over the parlor shown right also features a dentilled cornice and full-height paneling with rectilinear moldings. In this case they are painted yellowish white. The use of different color schemes to give individual character to architecturally identical or similar rooms was a common practice in grander houses during the second half of the 18th century. The contrast is heightened by an elaborately patterned carpet and a more decorative chimneypiece.

THE GEORGE WYTHE HOUSE

BELOW Although wallpapers or, in the grandest households, silk wall hangings, were used in lieu of painted plaster or wooden paneling in many Colonial homes during the second half of the 18th century, this was less often the case in dining rooms. Part of the reason was that, as in England, a more austere, masculine style of decoration was generally considered appropriate for dining rooms; fabrics and papers (especially flocked papers) also tended to retain the smells of food. The dining room at the George Wythe House has whitewashed walls and crisply contrasting mid-green-painted woodwork.

LIKE THE GOVERNOR'S PALACE (see pp.40–1), the George Wythe House (also located in Colonial Williamsburg, Virginia) can fairly claim to be steeped in American history. George Wythe, the original owner, was a lawyer and the first Professor of Law in the United States; he was first among the state signatories on the Declaration of Independence, and his residence served as headquarters to George Washington just before the Siege of Yorktown in 1781. Later, the house was to accommodate the General Assembly delegate Thomas Jefferson and his family.

The four-up, four-down, two-story residence was erected in the mid-1750s by Wythe's father-in-law, a local builder and planter named Richard Taliaferro. Probably the most handsome Colonial house in Williamsburg, it is brick-built (the bricks laid in Flemish bond above the water table) and has symmetrically arranged sash windows, a fireplace in each of the principal rooms, and extensive gardens. Outdoors are found a well and various outbuildings, including a smokehouse, kitchen, laundry, poultry house, lumber house, dovecote, and stables.

The Williamsburg Foundation, which acquired the property in 1938, faced a considerable challenge when restoring the house because by then there were few structural markers left to indicate the original function or decoration of particular rooms. For example, wall paneling – a good indicator of a room's status – was largely absent. Indeed, documentary evidence revealed that Richard Taliaferro had not specified any in his original plans. Consequently, the restorers, who also drew on contemporary paintings and engravings for reference, concluded that wall hangings – which became fashionable in more affluent Colonial households from the mid-18th century on – had been employed in many of the principal rooms.

Refurnished and redecorated in the early 1990s, the house thus features a number of documentary wallpapers displaying patterns and colors in vogue at the time of George Wythe's residency. These are supported by similarly sourced reproduction upholstery fabrics, and by woodwork painted in colors matched, through paint analysis, to the few original samples that have survived over two centuries.

ABOVE The walls of the northeast bedchamber of the George Wythe House are decorated with a boldly striped wallpaper inspired by one depicted in a contemporary hand-colored mezzotint engraving. The wooden chimneypiece has been painted yellowish white to match the paler stripe; the darker stripe is echoed in the colors of the chintz used for the bed hangings and the armchair.

BELOW The initial redecoration of the hallway and staircase at the George Wythe House was relatively austere. Whitewashed walls and flat-painted woodwork underlined the functional role of this part of the house, and were in keeping with many documented Colonial interiors. Following further historical research, however, they were replaced by the more flamboyant decorations seen above right.

ABOVE The mid-1990s redecoration of the foyer and stairway at the George Wythe House used blue and white documentary wallpaper with an elaborate pattern – interlinked vases, urns, pictorial cartouches, and scrolling foliage – that would also have been the height of fashion in Europe in the Colonial era. Such wallpapers were imported to the United States from England or France.

LEFT This view from the parlor through the hall and into the dining room illustrates the diversity of patterns and colors available on later 18th-century wallpapers. While the design of the hallway paper is inspired by Classical Roman wall paintings, the bold floral red and pink pattern in the parlor is European *chinoiserie*. The contrasting colors and patterns give each of the rooms a distinctive character and play a "zoning" role in the house.

WETHERSFIELD

FOUNDED IN 1644 on the Connecticut River, Wethersfield
is one of the oldest communities in the United States.
For 150 years it thrived as a center of regional commerce
and as a busy inland port that traded directly with the West
Indies. In the 19th century, however, the town's fortunes
dwindled after the river became unnavigable. Bypassed by
the industrial age, Wethersfield slid into rural obscurity – a
development that helped insure the survival of most of its
Colonial houses. Indeed, thanks to the efforts of bodies
such as the Connecticut Society of Colonial Dames, it is
now one of the best-preserved Colonial towns.

Three of the best examples of the substantial Colonial
houses built for families who prospered in Wethersfield
during the second half of the 18th century now make up
the Webb-Deane-Stevens Museum. The Joseph Webb
House was built in 1752, and is named after its original
owner, a local merchant. It is wood-framed, sheathed in
clapboard, and laid out in classic "four-over-four"

Georgian style, with spacious center halls and a story-and-
a-half attic (originally slave quarters) set under a gambrel
roof. Other notable architectural features include a
Classical entrance porch and "twelve-over-twelve" sliding
sash windows. The importance of the house as a guide to
Colonial style has undoubtedly been enhanced by the fact
that George Washington stayed there in May 1781 to plan
with the French commander, the Comte de Rochambeau,
the defeat of the English forces at Yorktown – the

ABOVE The walls of the upper hallway at Webb House display the classic tripartite division of frieze-cornice, field, and dado. The first and last, like the door and window frame, are painted a gray-green hue, while the field is contrasted in white (which may have originally been muted by the addition of a little charcoal-black or lampblack).

RIGHT Various tones of pink were used in Colonial houses from the 1720s on. The reddish-pink door and wall paneling seen here are in the Washington Bedchamber of the Webb House. The Rococo wallpaper dates to *c*.1752–3. The shades of brown in it would also have been a reddish-pink tone, but have darkened over time.

LEFT A "shell-domed" cupboard was built into the fireplace wall in the North Parlor. Its internal color scheme – blue, reddish orange , and gold – is typical of this feature, which is found in many grand late Colonial houses.

concluding battle of the American Revolution. Its real significance, however, lies in the various alterations and restorations that have been undertaken since then. Many of the rooms refurbished just after the World War I by the then owner Wallace Nutting were initially and erroneously redecorated in what is now known as Colonial Revival style (see pp.50–1). The rooms seen here, however, were redecorated during the late 20th century using the authentic Colonial palette and are furnished accordingly.

RIGHT The decorations and furniture of the best parlor in the Isaac Stevens House appear as they would have in the early 19th century. Contrasted with whitewashed plaster walls and ceiling, the subtle grayish tone evident in the painted wooden paneling is an example of one of the stone colors that became fashionable toward the end of the Colonial period.

BELOW Wall paneling, cornice, doors, window frames, and shutters in the Isaac Stevens dining parlor are all painted a pale green. The dining furniture includes painted "fancy" country chairs with woven rush seats. These are original to the house, probably made locally in Connecticut, and characteristic of modest, middle-class Colonial homes of the period. The transfer-printed blue and white tableware is English.

Completed in 1766, the Silas Deane House is, through association with its original owner, steeped in America's Revolutionary past. Lawyer Silas Deane, who had married Joseph Webb's widow, was Wethersfield's representative in the General Assembly of Connecticut. After election to the Continental Congress in Philadelphia in 1774, he went on to develop the United States Navy and to broker vital French support for the war with the British. Subsequently, he was accused of siphoning off French funding for munitions; he died in exile in Paris in 1787, but about 60 years later, his name was cleared by a Congressional Committee and his family was compensated.

Restored as nearly as possible to its appearance during his occupancy, the two-story, clapboard Silas Deane house is one of the most elegant buildings in Wethersfield. Its style is essentially Colonial Georgian, although the asymmetrical positioning of the front door, and the very wide entrance hall (which served as a room), appear to have been based on models seen in London and Paris, but not elsewhere in New England. Such features as the house's Chinese export porcelain and imported French and English upholstery fabrics are indicative of the increasing affluence and cultural sophistication of the colonial upper classes as independence beckoned.

The Isaac Stevens House was built in 1789 by a prosperous local saddler and tanner. The two-story building is typical Connecticut Georgian in style, but smaller and plainer than its more prestigious Webb and Deane neighbors, and only clapboarded on the front and side elevations – the back of the wooden frame is sheathed in cheaper, wide, butt-jointed boards. Inside, the architectural features (such as the wall paneling) are very similar to those in the other houses, but less elaborate. Similarly, the furniture, of which some 80 percent is original to the house, is simpler and more rustic. The Isaac Stevens House is thus very representative of a middle-class late Colonial home. The decorative palette is also particularly interesting because in some rooms the paler, grayish tones on the woodwork herald the arrival of colors that were to become fashionable during the early Federal period.

LEFT The wall paneling in the back parlor of the Silas Deane House is painted sage green. This green was most probably originally darker than it now appears, having faded over the passage of time as a result of regular exposure to daylight. The mid-18th-century mahogany table is accompanied by Queen Anne-style Connecticut chairs, also of mahogany. The yellow fabric used for the valance and the window drapes is wool, and its color is echoed in the upholstered chair seats.

LEFT Boldly patterned and colored upholstery fabrics became increasingly fashionable in Colonial houses during the second half of the 18th century and made a major contribution to the overall decorative palette. This upholstered wing-armchair in a corner of the North Bedchamber of the Isaac Stevens House displays a bold plant-form pattern, predominantly floral and embellished with birds, that shows distinct Chinese influence. The 18th-century mahogany table is English.

ABOVE The kitchen chamber of the Silas Deane house is painted off-white with contrasting bluish and greenish tones on the woodwork. In contrast to the other rooms in the household, the decoration is notably plain and functional – a reflection of the fact that this area would have been occupied by slaves kept to do the cooking, cleaning, and laundry. The crude sleeping pallet in the corner is explained by the fact that New England slaves invariably slept under the same roof as their owners.

A COLONIAL REVIVAL

RIGHT When the Connecticut Society of Colonial Dames bought the Joseph Webb House from the previous owner Wallace Nutting in 1919, the kitchen and dining room were set up as a tearoom to raise money for what became a museum. The redecoration of the rooms is not in authentic Colonial style. The mid-blue that was used is – like pale gray, pale green, white, and various off-whites – a typical Colonial Revival color of the early 20th century.

ABOVE The Colonial Revival mid-blue in the Webb House tearoom is more luminous than the mid-blues of the 18th century. The latter were either more muted (due to mixing charcoal black with Prussian blue) or had a distinct greenish tinge (from the addition of a little yellow ocher in the mix).

THE FIRST AMERICAN INTERNATIONAL trade fair, the Philadelphia Centennial Exposition of 1876, attracted some 10 million visitors to the city's Fairmount Park. While the exposition's major success – the Machinery Hall, with its portentous symbols of the country's imminent industrial rise – looked to the future, its eclectic display of historic buildings can be credited with fueling a widespread renewal of interest in the architectural past. The ensuing Colonial Revival movement, which manifested itself in the reconstruction and restoration of numerous Colonial houses in cities and towns such as Williamsburg (see pp.40–3) and Wethersfield (see pp.44–7), endures to this day. In terms of recreating authentic period interiors, however, this process was from the very beginning beset by two substantial problems.

The first of these centered on the fact that, prior to the development of microchemical paint analysis, even the most diligent researchers had to rely on visual assessment alone to identify original paint colors and finishes – an approach that sometimes proved to be rather unreliable.

The second difficulty lay in the fact that, during the process of turning many Colonial homes into museums, the desire for period authenticity was sometimes compromised by the preconceptions or the personal objectives of those in charge of the restorations.

One such early 20th-century restorer-curator was the Reverend Dr. Wallace Nutting, a commercial photographer, antiquarian, and entrepreneur as well as a minister, who owned the Joseph Webb House in Wethersfield, Connecticut (see pp.44–5), from 1916 to 1919. Architecturally, the four-up, four-down, three-story Webb House was well-documented, and most of its original architectural features were still intact when Nutting acquired it. However, he proceeded to make a number of significant changes, notably the removal of two second-floor windows, an attic-level overhang, and an internal staircase, and the installation of a new chimneypiece and new wall paneling imported from other Colonial houses. Nutting, confidently endorsing his own point of view, asserted: "The acquisition of old paneling and its installation in rooms that perhaps never had any, is legitimate. If the dwelling is substantial, there is nothing but praise in the effort to give it a good old dress."

Needless to say, the finer nuances of authentic period color were not of paramount concern to a wholesale revisionist such as Nutting. For example, for the walls of one of the Webb House parlors, which had originally been either flat-painted or wallpapered, he commissioned patriotic commemorative murals depicting the meeting between George Washington and the Comte de Rochambeau, the French commander, that took place on the premises in 1781, prior to the battle of Yorktown.

Such decorative features were an attractive draw for tourists and enhanced the photographic vignettes of the interiors sold by the commercially opportunistic Nutting. However, together with his use of a decorative palette that was notably paler than that employed in 18th-century interiors, they did much to disseminate historically dubious notions about Colonial decoration – to the extent that even now many people's perception of Colonial style is informed by these and similar early 20th-century restorations.

Nevertheless, we should not be too critical of Nutting. He saved the Webb House at a time when it might have been lost to posterity, and he established its viability as a museum. Moreover, although the changes he instigated have been put right by the current curators, they are regarded as representative of many early 20th-century Colonial revivals that have now collectively acquired the status of a legitimate historical style in their own right. As the architectural restorer Noel Hume pointed out in the 1960s: "People [now] realize that very rarely did anyone furnish a house or even a room totally to one period."

BELOW The "Yorktown Parlour" at the Webb House, as decorated by Wallace Nutting in 1916–19, with white-painted Colonial Revival paneling and one of the three murals commissioned by Nutting to reinforce the house's association with the Battle of Yorktown and the end of the Revolutionary war. Scientific paint analysis has revealed that the walls were originally green.

*"Wallace
Nutting…
the man who
looked back
and saw the
future…"*

(Edie Clark, writer)

LEFT The Southeast Chamber of
the Joseph Webb House was
redecorated in the 1960s in the
style of Wallace Nutting's earlier
20th-century Colonial Revival
refurbishment. The medium-to-
dark Prussian blue used on the
woodwork is closely matched to
the dark floral and faunal motifs
in the wallpaper, a hand-blocked
reproduction of an original 18th-
century paper. It is also echoed
in the chintz bed hangings, which
were duplicated from a scrap of
fabric that had survived in the
Isaac Stevens House next door.

Using the Colonial palette

Color was notable by its absence in the earliest colonial homes, most surfaces being either natural wood or simply whitewashed. Once the colonies had moved beyond a pioneer existence, however, the decorative palette became markedly more colorful. In New England, decoration largely mirrored English early Georgian taste (see pp.30–5). In wealthier households, expensive (often imported) pigments such as Prussian blue, vermilion, and verdigris were employed to produce a range of strong, saturated blue and green tones, sometimes enhanced with gilding. In less affluent homes and in rural areas where imported pigments were not always available, a variety of warm, more muted hues derived from local clays, soils, plants, and even animal blood were used. Examples included yellow-ocher, cane yellow, pinkish red and sage green.

ABOVE & RIGHT The banqueting hall at the rebuilt Governor's Palace, Colonial Williamsburg, shown before redecoration (above) and as it is now, recreating the style of Lord Botetourt's residency during the 18th century. The plain, deep frieze above the dentilled cornice is flat-painted in one of the earthy, reddish-brown hues popular throughout the Colonial period. The paler gray, beige, and off-white tones of the floral-patterned wallpaper on the frieze are representative of the paler tones that became increasingly fashionable toward the end of the Colonial era.

ABOVE, LEFT & BELOW White lead and/or charcoal black was mixed with indigo or Prussian blue to produce various blues. Many pinks were made by mixing white lead with red iron oxide or vermilion.

BELOW Vermilion- and red iron oxide-based pink paints were shaded with charcoal black, yellow-ocher and/or umber.

RIGHT Various tints of Colonial green were made with Prussian blue and ocher, black and ocher, or verdigris and white lead.

LEFT & ABOVE Pale yellows were mixed primarily from yellow-ocher and white lead. Mid-browns often contained red iron oxide, yellow-ocher, sienna, umber, calcium carbonate, and white lead.

BELOW The red- or yellow-brown tones of hardwood furniture made a major contribution to the color schemes in Colonial houses. Walnut and rosewood were popular during this time.

LEFT & BELOW Red iron oxide was a fashionable color for clapboard exteriors. The cost of pigments such as Prussian blue meant that they were used only on the front of many Colonial houses.

CROWN EXPRESSIONS
Imperial Cream • IMC–1

DULUX COLOUR SELECTOR
Natural Wheat

FIRED EARTH/
PAINT PORTFOLIO
Pompeian Red

WILLIAMSBURG
Weatherburn's Pale Blue

PAINT LIBRARY
Blue Blood

SANDERSON SPECTRUM
Fleet Blue • 55–6U

WILLIAMSBURG
Raleigh Tavern
Green Medium

WILLIAMSBURG
Raleigh Tavern
Green

WILLIAMSBURG
Purdie House Gray

Rococo style

LEFT The ornamentation of the majestic organ at the Wieskirche, constructed in 1745–54 near Munich, is highly characteristic of German Rococo. The dazzling combination of trelliswork, S- and C-scrolls, delicately scrolling foliage, and shell motifs, all worked in white-painted stone and plaster, and highlighted with gold leaf, might have been conceived by a pastry chef.

ABOVE *Rocaille* motifs, known as *muschelwerk* in Germany, are a recurring theme in Rococo interiors. Their dynamic, curvaceous shapes – as here at the Regnaholm Manor House near Orebro, Sweden – appeared like scrolling foliage forms and were well suited to an asymmetrical style of ornament.

THE ROCOCO STYLE emerged in France in the early 18th century in reaction to the heavy classicism and excessive formality of Baroque architecture and decoration as promoted at Louis XIV's Palace of Versailles and fashionable throughout most of his reign (1643–1715). The term Rococo was derived from the French word *rocaille*, the decorative shells and rocks used to cover the surfaces of ornamental grottoes, and it was these dynamic, asymmetrical forms (especially scallop shells), together with scrollwork (notably S- and C-scrolls), naturalistic sprigs of flowers, and sinuously undulating foliage, that provided the ornamental basis of Rococo style. Often combined with exotic *chinoiserie* imagery and thematic ornament, such as the Elements and the Four Seasons, and rendered in a palette of gold, white, ivory, cream, and pastel blues, greens, pinks, and yellows, French Rococo certainly provided light relief from the Baroque. Moreover, the impact of Rococo decoration was often multiplied by an extensive use of wall-hung mirrors – a decorative convention, promoted at Versailles, that also made a significant contribution to the overall lightness and airiness of the style.

From Sweden in the north to Portugal in the south, Rococo-style decoration was assimilated within the indigenous architectural traditions of many European states. For example, during the 1730s Rococo reached the Catholic German-speaking countries, where French elegance easily blended with an already highly theatrical architectural tradition. The Wieskirche, near Munich, built by Dominikus Zimmermann in 1745 and decorated by his elder brother Johann Baptist, perhaps represents German Rococo at its richest and most eloquent. G.W. von Knobelsdorff's pink and white Sans Souci Palace (see p.56), built at Potsdam in 1745 and executed to Frederick the Great's own plans, also incorporates significant Rococo elements alongside elements of Baroque.

ABOVE This bedroom alcove at the Regnaholm Manor House, built in the early 1760s near Orebro, illustrates how the flamboyant French Rococo style emerged in Sweden looking cooler and more restrained. The curving forms and motifs central to the style are presented in a more muted Swedish palette.

LEFT & BELOW Most of the
mid-18th-century Rococo
decorations at the Regnaholm
Manor House, near Orebro in
Sweden, have survived. This is
largely due to the fact that the
house has been mainly
unoccupied since World War I.
As in the bedroom alcove
(opposite) and the Chinese
Cabinet Room (below), the walls
of the salon (left) are lined with
canvas painted with Rococo
panels comprising C-scrolls and
intertwined foliage.

LEFT The library in G.W. von Knobelsdorff's Sans Souci Palace at Potsdam was built in 1745. The gilded scrollwork ornament applied over pastel-colored plaster is quintessential Rococo, as is the finely figured hardwood veneer paneling on the field of the walls. The use of large mirrors is also highly characteristic of the style.

BELOW The curving forms that lie at the heart of the Rococo style are clearly evident in the facade of the Château de Morsan. This Louis XV summer house and hunting lodge, now owned by Lillian Williams, was built c.1736 in Normandy, France.

RIGHT The *boiseries* in the main salon at the Château de Morsan are painted grayish-blue, with gilding used to highlight the Rococo-style moldings. This light and airy color combination is typical of French Rococo, as is the decorative convention of using mirror glass in upper door panels.

The ornate 17th-century Baroque style lived on in the richness of color and density of its ornament that survived in Teutonic 18th-century Rococo.

The Rococo style, essentially one of decoration rather than of architecture, was particularly suited to the design and embellishment of furniture, porcelain, metalwork, and fabrics. It was introduced to and disseminated throughout France by interior designers and *ornamentistes* such as Jean Bérain, Germain Boffrand, Gilles-Marie Oppenord, Juste-Aurèle Meissonnier, Jean Pillement, and Nicolas Pineau – the salons of the Hôtel de Soubise in Paris, by Boffrand, are an outstanding example of the style. The publication of numerous engravings of Rococo ornament helped in its wide dissemination through France and beyond.

In some parts of France, the Rococo style remained fashionable until the late 1780s, but elsewhere – notably in England where, as in North America, it had never been particularly well received in the first place – it was subject to increasing criticism from the middle years of the 18th century on. Originally considered lighthearted and joyful, it was now deemed simply frivolous and capricious.

Just as the Baroque had been ousted by the Rococo, so the Rococo, in turn, gave way to Neoclassicism (see pp.60–115). However, its seductive, delicate style of ornament and its predominantly pastel-colored, gilded palette, was to prove attractive and even compelling for later generations. Not only did the Rococo style enjoy a notable revival in the 19th century (even in the United States), but it also prepared the ground for the seeding and growth of the Art Nouveau movement that flowered in the late 19th and early 20th centuries.

ABOVE Exotic *chinoiserie* patterns and motifs were an important ingredient of Rococo style and were often interwoven with naturalistic sprigs of European foliage and flowers. The *chinoiserie* patterns on the bed hangings and upholstered chairs and on the painted furniture and stenciled walls in this bedroom at the Château de Morsan, are inspired by 17th- and 18th-century blue and white Delftware.

Using the Rococo palette

Gold is the indispensable and ubiquitous color of the Rococo palette. It is primarily used to define the scrollwork, shell motifs, and other curvaceous carvings, moldings, and patterns that are the heart of the style. When gold leaf proved too expensive, or was unavailable, yellow-gold paint was an acceptable substitute. The favored background colors are pastel blues, greens, pinks, and yellows; ivory, cream, and white; and the lustrous brown tones of finely figured hardwoods. More saturated hues include the purple-blue *(bleu lapis)*, green *(vert)*, and pink *(Pompadour rose)* of Sèvres porcelain (also found in Gobelin tapestries).

LEFT In the Imperial Palace of Schönbrunn, Vienna, the Millionen Room – named because of the huge sum spent on its decoration – is a compelling Austrian variant of French Rococo. Beneath a ceiling decorated with delicate, pastel-colored sprigs of flowers, are finely figured, rosewood-paneled walls with inlaid Persian miniatures and gilded S- and C-scrolls.

ABOVE & RIGHT The moldings on the chateau doors above are picked out against a pastel grayish-blue ground coat – a classic French Rococo color. In contrast, the way the carved motifs are defined against a white ground on the church organ (right) is typically German Rococo. Gilding, a key component of Rococo decoration, was primarily employed to highlight the characteristic curving, scrolling, and undulating ornament that underpins the style.

ABOVE & LEFT Floral- and foliage-patterned fabrics played a major role in the decor of Rococo interiors, especially in bedrooms, and the pastel blue and green hues of these chintzes were core colors of the French Rococo palette. A primary source of inspiration was the exotic Oriental compositions displayed on Chinese lacquerwares. Native European plants were also popular and usually displayed as sprigs or gently undulating stems.

ABOVE This royal bedroom in the Queluz Palace, Portugal, was decorated in 1760 and is a fine example of Portuguese Rococo.

RIGHT Empress Maria Theresa had the Vieux-Laque Room at the Imperial Palace of Schönbrunn redecorated *c.*1770 in honor of her recently deceased husband. Black lacquer panels were set into the walnut panels within gilt frames. The dark colors, which are remote from Rococo's pastel beginnings, demonstrate the adaptability of the style.

LEFT Pastel blues and pinks are employed behind the extravagant Rococo tracery in the library at the Sans Souci Palace, Potsdam. However, the dominant colours here are the golden browns of hardwood veneers, and vibrant, lustrous gilding.

DULUX HERITAGE
White

JOHN OLIVER
Imperial Yellow

CROWN EXPRESSIONS
Mustard • Spice MS–9

SANDERSON SPECTRUM
Bronze Brown • 57–6U

RALPH LAUREN PAINT
SOUTHPORT COLLECTION
Oar Lock • SO02C

FARROW & BALL
Suffield Green • U/C32

LAWRENCE T. BRIDGEMAN
Village Tavern Blue

J.W. BOLLOM & CO. LTD
NATURAL COLOR SYSTEM
S 3030–R70B

DULUX HERITAGE COLOURS
GEORGIAN (1714–1837)
Georgian 26

Neoclassical style

LEFT The early 19th-century Boscobel mansion in New York is representative of the then fashionable Federal style of architecture, characterized by a restrained use of exterior ornament. Like many Federal-style houses, Boscobel is woodframe and clapboard – the latter painted sand yellow and contrasted with the white finish on the rest of the woodwork.

ABOVE Designer Lena Proudlock's decoration of her late 18th-century farmhouse in Gloucestershire, England, is a late 20th-century pastiche of Swedish Gustavian style. The Gustavian palette of cool, flat colors is applied against a background of appropriately gilded Neoclassical moldings.

P ARTLY PROMPTED BY a growing disenchantment with the frivolity of the Rococo style (see pp.54–9), but also founded on a major revival of interest in the architecture, ornament, and decoration of Classical antiquity, Neoclassicism emerged around the middle of the 18th century and endured in a variety of guises until the mid-19th century. In the course of this period, it was to become not only a pan-European movement – its influence stretching from Scandinavia in the north down to the Iberian peninsula – but also the primary source of architectural and decorative inspiration for the newly independent United States across the Atlantic.

Underpinning the rise of Neoclassicism was the discovery and archeological exploration of a number of important Classical Greek and Roman sites in Italy, Greece, and Asia Minor – two of the most notable being Herculaneum and Pompeii, where excavations began in 1738 and 1755, respectively. The tremendous volume of new information on Greco-Roman architecture, ornament, furniture, and decoration unearthed at these locations provided the historical reference material for the Neoclassicists. The widespread dissemination of that material can be attributed to a number of complementary factors. First and foremost, many architects, designers, aesthetes, and affluent tourists went to view these sites in person (usually as part of a "Grand Tour" of the cultural capitals of Europe, such as Rome, Florence, and Athens); while for those unable to view the antiquities at first hand, a proliferation of publications – written accounts, architectural pattern books, paintings, prints, and engravings – provided an almost equally enlightening alternative. Particularly influential in this context were the writings and engravings of the Italian architect, archeologist, art dealer, and engraver Giovanni Battista Piranesi (1720–78), which detailed not only Greek and Roman buildings and artifacts, but also

ABOVE The architectural configuration and the contemporary decoration of the hallway of a London house is typical of the Regency style adopted in upper-middle-class homes during the early 19th century. Typically, a strong, flat wall color is contrasted with white balusters and ceiling.

LEFT The decorations and furniture in the Eating Room at Osterley Park, England, are the work of the Scottish architect and decorator Robert Adam. Elements of the Neoclassical Adam style include the Greek-style urn on a reeded plinth; the lyre motif in the chair back; and the stucco wall panels in which figurative roundels are framed by foliage and winged horses.

ABOVE Statuary, bas-reliefs, and stone-block and marble-panel walls at Jacques Garcia's chateau, Le Champ de Bataille, are modeled in the Neoclassical taste of late 18th-century France.

Etruscan and ancient Egyptian examples. A further and significant influence on the promotion of Neoclassicism in the late 18th and early 19th centuries were the Napoleonic Wars, in the course of which a French variant of Neoclassicism – known as Empire style (see below) – was "exported" across national borders in the wake of Napoleon Bonaparte's military conquests.

Given the tremendous richness and diversity of the Greco-Roman vocabulary of architecture, decoration, and ornament, Neoclassicism was inevitably subject to different interpretations and preferences which, in turn, gave rise to a number of related but distinct Neoclassical styles. For example, in France (see pp.64–9) the Louis XVI style, or *"goût antique,"* was largely inspired by Piranesi's designs and the work of Robert Adam (see below). Fashionable from the early 1770s until Louis' execution by guillotine in 1793, and also the basis of Swedish Gustavian style during that period (see pp.106–15), it was supplanted during the last five years of the 18th century by the more austere

Directoire style based on Greek rather than Roman prototypes. Under the rule of Napleon Bonaparte this was, in turn, superseded by the majestic and colorful Empire style, which combined Imperial Roman imagery and decoration with ancient Egyptian and military motifs.

In England, Adam style (see pp.70–7), generated by the work of Scottish architect Robert Adam (1728–92), dominated the second half of the 18th century. Drawing on the architectural forms of Roman antiquity and the Italian Renaissance and sympathetically combining them with ancient Greek and Etruscan decorative motifs, Adam style not only provided inspiration for the Louis XVI style, but also, prior to the advent of the Empire-based English Regency style (see pp.78–81), made a major impact in Italy (see pp.82–5), and influenced the early Neoclassical movement in North America.

With the exception of an Italian, Piranesi, it could be argued that French and British architects led the way in developing and promoting the Neoclassical styles – French

ABOVE In one of the principal bedrooms of the Palacio Real de Aranjuez, until the early 20th century the Spanish monarchy's springtime residence south of Madrid, the combination of strong colors and formally structured Classical floral motifs redolent of Empire-style decoration pervades the upholstery fabrics. Equally characteristic is the Spanish hardwood furniture with ebony and gilt decorative details.

Empire style, for example, also became highly fashionable in Spain during the early 19th century (see pp.86–93). However, the country that probably took Neoclassicism closest to its heart was the United States. There is no doubt that the historical parallels – drawn by such influential figures as Thomas Jefferson, third President of the United States (1801–9) – between the newly independent, democratic American republic and ancient Greece (the birthplace of democracy) and the old Roman republic gave additional resonance to the new nation's adoption and adaptation of, in turn, the Adam-based and Imperial Roman Federal styles, Empire style, and during the 1830s and 1840s, a Greek Revival (see pp.94–105).

ABOVE & RIGHT French Empire style was the inspiration for the decoration and furnishing of antique dealer Bernd Goeckler's New York apartment in the late 1990s. In this living room and adjacent bedroom, flat-painted yellow walls provide an appropriately harmonious backdrop for gilded moldings derived from the Classical vocabulary of ornament and reddish-brown mahogany and ebonized Empire furniture.

ABOVE In a corner of another living room in Bernd Goeckler's apartment, flat-painted yellow walls again provide an appropriate period background for Empire furniture and a regimented display of prints and engravings typical of early 19th century interiors. The subject matter of the art works – ruins and archeological sites from Classical antiquity, and the Sphinx – reflect the cultural preoccupations of the Neoclassicists and Napoleon's military campaign in Egypt.

A NORMANDY CHATEAU

RIGHT The red and white check fabric employed in this top-floor bedroom at the Château de Morsan is a modern reproduction of a French fabric fashionable during the later years of the 18th century. It is used on the chairs and for the window, bed, and wall hangings. The overall lightness of the color scheme, which is fairly typical of late 18th-century bedrooms, is achieved by contrasting the fabric with a white-painted ceiling and woodwork and natural pine furniture and floorboards.

BELOW Striped fabrics also became fashionable in French Neoclassical interiors. The green and white fabric used for the hangings, cover, and bolsters of a carved and painted Louis XVI bed is a document of a late 18th-century original.

LOCATED IN NORMANDY, France, the Château de Morsan was built *c.*1765 during the reign of Louis XV (1715–74). Although sometimes used as a hunting lodge, it was conceived and employed primarily as a *maison de plaisance*, or summer house. It has recently been restored and refurnished by its owner Lillian Williams, an international authority on French period fabrics and decoration.

The chateau is particularly interesting in terms of the development of architectural and decorative styles in France during the later years of the 18th century. Specifically, it reflects the gradual transition from the curvaceous, often flamboyant Rococo style that dominated most of the reign of Louis XV to the more restrained, rectilinear Neoclassical style (or "*goût antique*") that flourished under Louis XVI (reigned 1774–92).

For example, the exterior of the chateau – especially the roof line, window heads, doors, and shutters and the balcony of the principal facade – displays the curved forms typical of the Rococo style. These are also evident in the gilded moldings on the glazed doors in the entrance hall. In contrast, the *boiseries* in many rooms feature gilded or painted moldings that are typically Neoclassical in their simple profile and rectilinear configuration.

Such contrasts are equally apparent in the chateau's furniture. Most of the beds, for example, are elaborate *lits à la polonaise*. Incorporating domed canopies secured with curved, fabric-covered rods attached to the corner-posts, and named in honor of Louis XV's Polish wife Maria Karolina Leszczynska, they first appeared in French Rococo bedrooms during the mid-18th century and remained fashionable in early Neoclassical interiors. Rococo taste is also displayed in various Louis XV tables, desks, and chairs featuring the extravagantly curved cabriole legs characteristic of the style. Conversely, many of the chateau's other chairs and stools, some daybeds, and numerous columnar plinths used to display busts and other statuary date to Louis XVI and exhibit the straighter, more austere lines of Neoclassicism.

LEFT The delicate, floral patterns popularized in France by Queen Marie Antoinette are exemplified by the fabric employed for the valance, drapes, and daybed. The yellow is echoed on the walls and in the secondary drapes.

RIGHT Typically, stronger colors are employed in reception rooms. In the entrance hall a dark green provides the ground color for the wall paneling and is enriched with gilt moldings.

BELOW White and pale pink provide the ground colors in this bedroom. Striped fabrics and floral wall paneling are harmoniously juxtaposed by using similar tones of green.

Not surprisingly, the fabrics chosen by Lillian Williams also accurately mirror the changing styles of the second half of the 18th century, a period in which exotic, often bold Rococo floral patterns, mostly of Chinese origin, were eventually superseded by smaller, more delicate floral imagery of European origin, and by geometric patterns of stripes and checks. Equally characteristic of the period are the various color schemes she has employed. Stronger, more saturated hues, often contrasted and enlivened with gilding, include dark green, mauve-blue, rust-red and vibrant yellow. Lighter colors, most evident in the bedrooms, include paler tones of green and milky yellows, almost invariably contrasted with white or grayish off-white. All are quintessentially French.

LEFT The Marble Hall at the Château du Champ de Bataille features a rich and diverse range of real marble and *faux marbre* architectural fixtures and fittings. Prominent among these are the geometric-pattern floor; the chimneypiece; the pilasters and columnar pedestals; and the tabletop. The metallic hues popular in Louis Seize interiors are evident in the bronze, brass, and gilded Classical motifs and imagery. The crimson-red color of the drapes is picked up in the wall hangings (and echoes the rust-red of the pilasters).

BELOW Cooler color schemes, such as the combination of pale gray and light blue in this bathroom, were also in vogue during the reign of Louis XVI.

CHATEAU DU CHAMP DE BATAILLE

RIGHT As in the bathroom above right, cool, pale tints of gray and blue are employed on the wall paneling of a bedroom. In this case they are, however, balanced by the warmer tones of red and pink in the bed and window hangings, the upholstered chair seats and backs, and the Oriental carpet. The patterns in these fabric furnishings are typical of the delicate, naturalistic floral designs popularized in France by Louis XVI's queen, Marie Antoinette, during the last quarter of the 18th century – their use being primarily confined to ladies' boudoirs.

LOCATED NEAR THE town of Le Neubourg in Normandy, France, the Château du Champ de Bataille was built for the Comte de Créqui in the late 17th century, a period in which the Baroque style was still flourishing in France. The chateau is, however, admired for its Neoclassical interiors, which were remodeled in the late 18th century during the reign of Louis XVI (1774–92). Subsequently restored to their original splendor by current owner Jacques Garcia, these interiors have, together with its parks and gardens, earned the chateau the accolade "the Norman Versailles."

In typical Louis Seize style, the interior architectural fixtures and fittings draw heavily on the Greco-Roman vocabulary of ornament, with considerable use of marble and painted *faux marbres*. The fabric furnishings, like the exceptionally fine furniture, also represent the height of period fashion – as do the various color schemes, which illustrate both the cooler and paler and the richer and darker palettes popular in late 18th-century France.

RIGHT The Porcelain Corridor at the Château du Champ de Bataille is employed to display an impressive collection of Imari and Chinese blue-and-white porcelain – both of which were exported to France in considerable quantities during the late 18th century. The colors chosen for the *boiseries* – dark red, dark blue, black, and gold – were inspired by the distinctive Imari palette. However, they are also redolent of Imperial Roman decoration and are precursors of the patriotic combination of red and blue (usually with white) favored for the Directoire style of the late 1790s.

FAR RIGHT A tremendous range and diversity of colors and patterns were available to French Neoclassical architects and decorators whose patrons could afford the cost of expensive polychromatic marbles and porphyries. Stoneware artifacts, modeled on Greco-Roman prototypes, were also, as here, a source of rich, saturated colors.

RIGHT & FAR RIGHT Cool grayed white and blue provide the ground colors for the *boiseries* in these bathrooms at the Château du Champ de Bataille. In the room on the left, the grayed white is carried over to the painted bergere chair and echoed in the zinc lining of the bathtub. It is balanced, however, by the warmer red and yellow tones of the bath canopy, wall hangings, and rug, and by the reddish-terracottta *faux marbre* finish on the side of the tub. In the bathroom on the right, the coolness of the grayed-blue background color is also moderated – but to a much lesser extent – by the brown hues of the hardwood furniture and parquet flooring, and the pale pink tones in the window hangings.

Using the French Neoclassical palette

Paler color schemes in French Neoclassical interiors were confined mainly to ladies' boudoirs. Pale tones of green and milky yellow, contrasted with white or light gray, were popular during the reign of Louis XVI, while subtle harmonies of pastel colors, notably grayed blues and violets, cream, and apricot, were favored for Empire style. Stronger color schemes fashionable under Louis XVI featured dark green, mauve-blue, rust-red and vibrant yellow, often enlivened with gilding. Under the Directoire, a patriotic palette of red, white, and blue, combined with deep green, violet, white, ivory, and gold, came into vogue. Deeper, strongly contrasted Empire colors included purple, lemon-yellow, and deep apple-green, complemented by strong pinks or reds and often set against white grounds and gilded motifs.

RIGHT A red and white check fabric of the kind popular in France under Louis XVI is lined with a paler floral pattern in the bed hanging and carried over as window drapes and wall hangings.

BELOW The use of darker colors was common in French Neoclassical interiors. Deep apple-green, purple-blue, and reddish terracotta feature in this opulent room.

ABOVE Fabrics were often used in French salons to soften the impact of rectilinear and sometimes rather austere Neoclassical architectural moldings. Here, red and pink patterned printed cotton chintz, floral silk damask and plain satin are deployed for the hangings and upholstery.

LEFT Dark green ground colors were fashionable in Louis XVI, Directoire, and Empire interiors. A variety of shades were produced, by employing pigments such as malachite, verdigris, *terre verte* (Verona green), and chromium oxide, often mixed with lampblack, vermilion, and lead white.

LEFT Extensive use of variegated marble and painted *faux marbre* in this entrance hall reflects the influence of Classical Roman architecture. Red and yellow Roman shades echo the reddish terracotta (Pompeiian red) of the double-doors and the yellow tones of the gilded door moldings, as well as the yellow *faux marbre* sections of wall.

RIGHT Architectural components made of variegated polychromatic marbles and porphyries featured prominently in grand French Neoclassical interiors, especially during the reign of Louis XVI.

DULUX COLOUR SELECTOR
Marshmallow

CROWN EXPRESSIONS
Soleil · SO–10

CROWN EXPRESSIONS
Mustard Spice · MS–9

CROWN COLOUR PLANNER
Orchestral Red

OLD VILLAGE PAINT
WILLIAMSBURG
2–2 Child's Rocker
Bright Red

ABOVE The stone colors of the statuary and the *trompe l'oeil* ceiling rosettes in the Egyptian Library at Le Champ de Bataille are enlivened by a pinkish-red carpet, pastel-pink upholstered chair seats, and Pompeiian-red and gilded end-wall panels.

RIGHT *Faux marbre* wall finishes were fashionable under Louis XVI. In the second-floor dining room of Le Champ de Bataille, a darker, umber-colored *faux marbre* is contrasted with a more lustrous painted simulation of Yellow Siena marble.

SANDERSON SPECTRUM
Northern Pine · 56–1U

RALPH LAUREN PAINTS
SOUTHPORT COLLECTION
Greens Farms · SO03B

LEFT Classical Roman decoration and Imari porcelain inspired the use of dark red and blue and black and gilded *boiseries* at Le Champ de Bataille.

RIGHT Tints of yellow-ocher, a more vibrant, chrome-based yellow, and white establish one of the lighter color schemes favored for late 18th-century bedrooms.

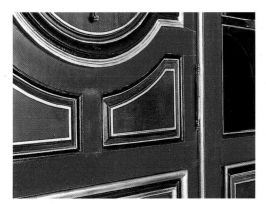

DULUX HERITAGE
Oxford Blue

JOHN OLIVER
Betty II Blue

ROBERT ADAM played a highly significant role in the development of Neoclassicism, not only in Britain, but also abroad (see pp.60–3). However, because there were relatively few building projects commissioned in Britain during the second half of the 18th century, the distinctive and influential Adam style he generated during this period was expressed mainly in the remodeling of houses.

Osterley Park, in Middlesex, is one of the finest surviving examples of this. Built in the 1570s, the house was owned by Francis Child, who commissioned Adam to reduce it in size and give it a more "modern" image. The work was carried out from the late 1750s to the mid-1760s, and the resulting interiors are eloquent expressions of Adam's quotations from, and reinterpretations of, the Classical vocabulary of architecture and ornament.

Throughout, motifs and imagery derived from Greek, Etruscan, Roman, and Italian Renaissance sources are eclectically combined. They are defined, often in white, against the Adam decorative palette comprising pale blues and greens; lilac, apricot, and opal tints; stronger, more saturated blue, green and terracotta; and gold. The effect is undoubtedly grand, but it is also light, elegant, harmonious, and full of imaginative virtuosity.

OSTERLEY PARK

ABOVE & FAR LEFT Worked on pale green and blue grounds, the wall and door decorations in the Etruscan Dressing Room were painted by Pietro Maria Borgnis on sheets of paper, which were cut out and pasted in position.

LEFT The rectilinear wall panels and circular ceiling medallions in the Eating Room feature scrolling foliage, winged Pegasuses, and other Classical motifs, picked out in white against a pale-green ground.

RIGHT The color scheme in the Hall, which also served as a receiving room, has been restored in white and greenish gray in accordance with a contemporary description of it.

*"Adam
produced
exquisite
interiors that
were at once
serene, elegant
and full of
imaginative
virtuosity."*

(James Stevens Curl,
architectural historian)

LEFT The Gallery at Osterley
Park was redecorated and
furnished by Robert Adam to
display the owner Francis Child's
extensive collection of gilt-
framed pictures. Some 132 feet
(40 meters) long, it was restored
in the late 1990s to Adam's color
scheme: the papered walls above
the dado are painted a pea-green
color, with the ceiling and its
molding white, and the walls
below the white dado rail lilac.

A LATE GEORGIAN TOWNHOUSE

THE CONTRIBUTING GARDENS EDITOR of *Country Life* magazine, Leslie Geddes-Brown, is the current owner of this brick-built, five-story, late Georgian townhouse in north London. The first of five houses constructed *c.*1800 in a Canonbury square by the property developer Henry Leroux, it had, by the 1960s, become semi-derelict. Initially renovated in the early 1970s, the interior has recently been restored by Geddes-Brown to its original Georgian layout and also redecorated with color schemes fashionable in England during the late 18th and early 19th centuries.

In comparison to the grandest English interiors of the period, such as those remodeled by Robert Adam at Osterley Park in Middlesex (see pp.70–3), there is a marked quality of reticence or modesty evident in the house's architecture and decoration – a characteristic of ordinary late 18th-century English townhouses, even substantial ones such as this. The profiles of the sash window, paneled door, baseboard, and cupboard moldings, for example, are relatively plain. Similarly, although some of the walls are finished with fashionable papers, most are flat-painted rather than decorated with elaborate stucco work, expensive silk hangings or handpainted Classical motifs and imagery, as at Osterley Park. Nevertheless, despite such

ABOVE & LEFT The walls of the garden room in the Canonbury townhouse are lined with a hutch (above) and full-height storage cupboards (left), both of which are built in and original. The fielded center panels of their doors are flat-painted a yellow-cream color, while the surrounding framework is painted gray – a color combination that serves to emphasize the simple, rectilinear configuration of typical late Georgian moldings.

differences of elaboration in the architectural and decorative details, the interiors of both houses display the clean lines and symmetry of proportion inherent in the late Georgian Neoclassical style – qualities that are characteristically enhanced by the decorative palette and numerous period furnishings.

In the decorative scheme, the paint colors in the Canonbury townhouse are derived mainly from the cooler side of the late Georgian palette, with a particular emphasis on cream, gray, and blue on the walls and original built-in hutches, cupboards, and bookcases. These elegant combinations provide an unobtrusive backdrop for various Georgian desks, chests, and occasional chairs made of finely figured hardwoods – notably mahogany, walnut, and satinwood. Further decorative coherence appropriate to the style and period is achieved in many of the rooms by matching the blue wall tones with upholstered armchairs and sofas, and with elements of floral-patterned Persian rugs – the latter typically laid over narrow, butt-jointed, bare pine floorboards.

FAR LEFT In the kitchen, a white plaster ceiling and pale blue plaster walls are subtly contrasted with a gray-painted built-in hutch. This color combination provides a tonally sympathetic backdrop to a display of 19th-century, blue-and-white transfer-printed pottery and porcelain. Prominent Neoclassical features include the corner rosettes and reeded jambs of the window frame. The butcher's block table is modern. However, it is made of beech – a hardwood that is a close tonal match to the original butt-jointed pine floorboards.

ABOVE & ABOVE RIGHT Pale, bluish-gray tones are employed on the walls and built-in bookcases in the large reception room on the *piano nobile*. They are coordinated with not only the blue upholstered armchair and the blue in the Persian rugs, but also the blue-gray tones of the variegated marble fireplace. Similar matches of hues and tone are evident between the various pieces of reddish-brown Georgian mahogany furniture, the floorboards, the pair of Regency obelisks flanking the hearth, and the red ground colors in the Persian rugs.

RIGHT A two-tone blue striped wallpaper has been hung in the study. Stripe patterns, for both papers and fabrics, came into vogue around the turn of the 18th century and were to become a core decorative element in Regency style (see pp.78–81).

ABOVE The understated elegance of late Georgian townhouses is founded on their architectural symmetry and decorative coherence – qualities that are immediately evident in the main room of the Canonbury townhouse. The room also conveys a tremendous and characteristic sense of light and space. This is partly due to the pale, bluish-gray tones of the painted walls and ceiling, but is founded on the restrained use of architectural moldings, the height of the ceiling, and, especially, the full-height, nine-over-nine sliding sash windows.

Using the Late Georgian palette

With the exception of some interiors (known as "Etruscan rooms") in which Classical motifs and moldings were picked out in the deep, reddish terracotta hue and black found on ancient Greek vases, the late Georgian palette is dominated by a combination of pale and vivid colors. Those favored by the highly influential Robert Adam (see pp.70–3) include pale and medium green; tints of lilac, pink, apricot, opal, and gray; and a stronger, more saturated range of green and blue. Particularly good sources of reference for the palette are Adam's original designs in the British Museum, and the ceramics made by Josiah Wedgwood – especially his Jasperware (a form of stoneware), the cool, pale colors of which were derived from ancient cameos.

LEFT At Osterley Park, Robert Adam used a flat-painted pea-green color on the walls. It was echoed in the set of upholstered furniture and contrasted with a lilac tint on the dado. The harmonious tonal relationship of these colors echoes the room's architectural coherence.

RIGHT In another room at Osterley Park, pale tints of green on the field and blue on the dado provide the ground colors for hand-painted Etruscan motifs. As in the room shown left, the green and blue are tonally matched.

LEFT Marble chimneypieces are a notable feature of grander late Georgian interiors. This example, at Osterley Park, is integrated into the the room's overall color scheme by finishing adjacent moldings, such as the dado rail, in a similar tone of white.

RIGHT In the Hall at Osterley Park, Adam used a light grayish tone as a painted ground for the plaster relief moldings. The darker, grayish-brown tones of the chimneypiece, and the bas-relief above it, are coordinated with the inlaid marble floor.

BELOW A wide range of tints and shades of blue were used in late Georgian interiors. This duotone blue striped wallpaper is an example of the stronger, more saturated blues that became more fashionable during the Regency period (see pp.78–81).

ABOVE & BELOW Built-in furniture such as storage cupboards and hutches, often installed in late-Georgian houses, were usually made of softwoods such as pine or fir and painted. In some cases, a single color was used; this gave less prominence to the decorative moldings, but enhanced the visual sense of space in a room. More often, either two colors or two shades of one color were employed. This had the effect of highlighting the decorative moldings – which in late Georgian-style interiors were invariably elegant, rectilinear, and derived from the Classical Orders of architecture.

LEFT Stoneware artifacts based on Greco-Roman prototypes feature in late-Georgian rooms.

BELOW & RIGHT Blue-gray tones complement period furniture and artwork.

PAINT MAGIC/
JOCASTA INNES
Lavender Grey

SANDERSON SPECTRUM
Maltese Grey • 45–11M

PAINT LIBRARY
Lavenham Blue

DULUX HERITAGE COLOURS
GEORGIAN (1714–1837)
Georgian 30

MARSTON & LANGINGER
Leaf Green

COLOURMAN
No. 120

FARROW & BALL
Dauphin • U/C18

DULUX HERITAGE COLOURS
GEORGIAN (1714–1837)
Georgian 17

ACE ILLUMINATIONS
Calaveras • 174–E

REGENCY INTERIORS

ALTHOUGH THE PERIOD of English history known as the Regency spanned the years 1811–20 – when George, Prince of Wales, ruled while his father George III was ill – the style of decoration, ornament, and, to a lesser degree, architecture that came to be known as Regency initially appeared in the late 1780s and remained fashionable for a decade after the end of the Prince's reign (as George IV) in 1830. Promoted by Prince George's enthusiasm for French design and culture, early Regency style mirrored the grand Neoclassical style fashionable in France from 1774 to 1792 during the reign of Louis XVI (see pp.60–9). Characterized by symmetrical compositions of fine-quality French furniture, fabrics, wallpapers, mirrors, and chandeliers – set against a backdrop of Greco-Roman columns, pilasters, friezes, and other Classical moldings – it was exemplified in England by the work of architect Henry Holland and, especially, the opulent, refined interiors that he designed for the Prince's Carlton House, in London.

By the late 1790s, however, Regency style had begun to evolve and, in so doing, became more distinctively English. French influence remained significant – specifically in the Empire style patronized by Napoleon Bonaparte and his Empress Josephine that was adopted across much of

Europe and United States during the early 19th century; the style was characterized by Imperial Roman decoration and ornament combined with Etruscan, Egyptian, and military forms and motifs. English architects, decorators, fabric and furniture makers, and ceramics factories did not, however, simply replicate French prototypes. Instead, "Gothick" architectural features, such as pointed arches and window tracery, were often assimilated within the style, as was *chinoiserie* decoration – the latter most notably in some of the extravagant interiors at the Brighton Pavilion, designed by Henry Holland and John Nash.

A further difference between the Empire and Regency styles lay in the fact that, while the former was invariably confined to wealthy French households, a modest version of Regency style was widely adopted in less affluent English homes. Fueling this democratization of decoration were periodicals such as Rudolph Ackermann's *The Repository of Art* (published 1809–28), which contained colored plates displaying not only the grandest Regency interiors, but also ideas for more practical schemes. These relied less on expensive fabrics and wallpapers, and more on relatively affordable flat-painted color, to establish the fundamental symmetry and coherence of Regency style.

ABOVE By enhancing the
architectural coherence of the
space, the recent redecoration of
this Regency room is true to the
spirit of Regency style. The bold,
tonally balanced combination
of greenish yellow and gray-
blue paint is sophisticated and
provides a harmonious backdrop
for artifacts and paintings.

ABOVE The hallway of the
south London Regency house
shown top also features a bold
color scheme, in which the red on
the walls, enriched by the
mahogany handrail of the
balustrade, is contrasted with a
white ceiling and balusters.

Using the Regency palette

Although white and paler colors such as cream and light gray were sometimes used, Regency style is characterized by stronger, more vivid hues. Notable examples, most evident in both textiles and flat-painted and papered wall finishes, include lilac and turquoise; deep pink, cherry, orange, crimson, and Pompeiian red; emerald green; and saffron and sulfur-yellows. Gilding is also employed, primarily on decorative moldings, and features most prominently in grander Regency interiors. All colors are invariably applied flat and opaque – distressing techniques such as ragging and sponging are an inauthentic, modern conceit.

LEFT Paler, more muted tones of yellow were also employed by Regency decorators – in the upholstery fabric on the settee, they are combined with pink, green, and off-white. Apart from the gilt moldings, other typical Regency colors on display include the predominantly gray and black hues of the columnar, variegated marble plinth and the lustrous brown tones of the mahogany secretary.

BELOW Bluish-gray bookcases are contrasted with white moldings.

ABOVE Striking counterpoints of color are typical of Regency interiors. Here a strong, saturated red on the walls is contrasted with white-painted woodwork. The elegant simplicity of the architecture and the decoration is underpinned by the natural wood tones of the clear-waxed pine floorboards, which extend from the hall to the adjacent rooms.

RIGHT Polychromatic stripe-pattern wallpapers and upholstery fabrics were fashionable in English Regency homes. Here, thinner pale yellow, pink, and grayish-blue stripes are alternated with wide black stripes that emphasize the bold rectilinear design.

FAR RIGHT Vibrant saturated yellows, often complemented by gilded moldings and set against a white ground, were used in grand Regency interiors.

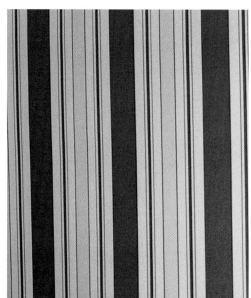

RIGHT On this drawing-room wallpaper, stylized foliate stripes are rendered in white against a lavender-blue ground. The gilt-framed convex mirror (or *girondole*) is an evocative Regency artifact.

BELOW LEFT, CENTER & RIGHT Regency decorators also used solid color (painted or in the form of plain papers). The most effective recreations of the style use strong, saturated colors such as the yellowish green, sandstone, and reddish orange here.

LEFT Large expanses of solid color applied to the walls of Regency rooms were often contrasted with white or off-white painted woodwork. However, more adventurous color combinations are also authentic. Here, the yellow on the walls is contrasted with lavender-blue doors and moldings. These colors are harmoniously juxtaposed because they are of equivalent tonal value – they absorb and reflect light in roughly equal measure.

LIZ INDUNI
TRADITIONAL PAINTS
Stone

THE CASA PAINT CO.
Tropics

SANDERSON SPECTRUM
Tahitian Gold • 7–24D

PAINT LIBRARY
Habana Gold

CROWN EXPRESSIONS
Etruscan Orange • EO–1

PAINT LIBRARY
Galway Blazer

RALPH LAUREN PAINT
SOUTHPORT COLLECTION
Black Rock Harbor • SO01D

BRATS LTD
MEDITERRANEAN PALETTE
Putnam Blue

ACE ILLUMINATIONS
Rock of Ages • 179–C

VILLA DI GEGGIANO

RIGHT The Neoclassical fireplace in the Green Salon was installed in the early 20th century by the present owner's grandfather, as part of the room's repair and redecoration following an earthquake. Its yellow Siena marble frieze and jambs are echoed in the painted *faux marbre* at the top of the dado. The mural on the field of the wall depicts scenes of the Italian countryside and is typical of the pastoral imagery popular in Europe in the late 18th century.

LEFT Alfieri's Bedchamber at the Villa di Geggiano is named in honor of the Italian poet and playwright Count Vittorio Alfieri (1749–1803), a frequent visitor. The furniture, marble floor, cornice, and wallpaper date to the remodeling in the 1780s.

ALTHOUGH ITALY, with its rich repository of Classical Roman ruins, was, together with ancient Greece, the mainspring and the primary source of reference for Neoclassicism, the style first flourished elsewhere in Europe. Perhaps by being too close to the source and possibly because living in a country steeped in cultural history can discourage stylistic innovation, Italian architects were generally followers of the Neoclassical style rather than its originators. In this context, the 16th-century Villa di Geggiano, near Siena, could be said to offer a fine example of leisurely historical continuity.

First inhabited by the Bandinelli family in 1527, the villa has remained fundamentally unchanged since being remodeled in the Neoclassical style in the late 1770s and early 1780s – a project that was prompted by a Bandinelli family wedding. Its restrained, symmetrical facade strikes a formal note in the context of the vernacular architecture of the surrounding Tuscan countryside (see pp.160–71). The beautifully decorated interiors, meanwhile, bear witness to the dedicated efforts of recent generations of

the Bandinelli family to retain an 18th-century Neoclassical decor and palette. For example, the father of the current occupant went to exceptional lengths to recover furniture, paintings, and fabrics that had become dispersed over the years. Using an old inventory, he was able to reinstall numerous items, most of which had survived their travels remarkably well. During World War II, the same enterprising Bandinelli saved the entire villa from destruction by the Nazis. His ploy was to assure them that the German poet, novelist, and playwright Johann Wolfgang von Goethe (1749–1832) had once stayed there (he had not), effectively turning the villa into an inviolable Aryan shrine.

Despite a few dashes of Rococo style (see pp.54–9), and a rather unsympathetic early 20th-century redecoration of the Green Salon ceiling (following an earthquake), the Villa di Geggiano endures in the spirit of Neoclassical reserve and taste. With its elegant frescoes, striking *trompe l'oeil* wallpapers, and fine furniture, it reflects a very Italian sense of familial continuity and cultural curatorship.

RIGHT The long entrance hall leading in from the gardens is decorated with frescoes by the itinerant Tyrolean artist Ignazio Moder. Their subject is a stylized Classical treatment of rural life and the Four Seasons. The frescoes are based on engravings by the Florentine artist Francesco Bartolozzi.

FAR RIGHT In the Villa di Geggiano's "Gossip Room," female guests seated on the long bench were able to assess the male guests who strolled up and down (discreetly assessing, in turn, the women). The Neoclassical decor, notably the painted panels on the walls and ceiling, is executed with delicacy.

ABOVE The hand-finished *papier peint* on the walls of the Blue Room, or *Saletta*, at the Villa di Geggiano was acquired from the Paris store Le Grand Balcon in 1770. Its monochromatic *trompe l'oeil* pattern, rendered in shades of blue, features tiers of Classical arcading. The blue tones of the paper are echoed in the painted moldings of the paneled door (which has a painted *faux marbre* frame) and on the furniture (painted by local artisans).

Using the Italian Neoclassical palette

For the most part, the Italian Neoclassical palette is softer than its French, English, and American counterparts. In these latter countries, Neoclassical decorators tended to make greater use of more saturated, vibrant hues but the pastel blue, pink, yellow, and gray that dominate the Italian palette are similar to the paler colors used in French Rococo style (see pp.54–9). The explanation for this partly resides in the Italian love of *grisaille*. Handpainted on plaster, paper, or canvas, this monochromatic form of *trompe l'oeil* relies on subtle tints and shades of the same basic color to create the illusion of three-dimensional architecture and plant forms.

LEFT Neoclassical Italian interiors use color and pattern to harmonize the furnishings and the decorations. In the Blue Room at the Villa di Geggiano, the motifs on the tables and chairs echo the design and hues of the handmade wallpaper.

BELOW Yellow-green walls provide the backdrop for Neoclassical double-doors surrounded by a *faux marbre* frame. The door moldings are in yellow-gold paint with pastel blue highlights.

ABOVE Stronger colors such as rust-red and olive-green tended to be used sparingly in Italian Neoclassical rooms, as on this paneled door embellished with a string of leaves centered on a faceted diamond motif.

RIGHT Real marble and painted *faux marbre* feature prominently in Italian Neoclassical decor. The yellow Siena marble of this fireplace and the *faux* Siena on the dado are characteristic of the style.

LEFT Yellow, yellowish-green, and reddish-brown hues contrast with white-painted plaster and grayish *faux marbre* baseboards in this late 18th-century Italian bedroom. The original wallpaper is patterned with a repeat floral motif set in vertical foliate stripes – a classic design of the period.

ABOVE The distinction between fine art and interior decoration was often blurred in Italian Neoclassicism. Flanked by green and gold painted furniture, a door features twin pastoral scenes.

ABOVE RIGHT A *trompe l'oeil* arched stone niche, flanked by *faux marbre* wall paneling, displays a Classical Roman urn. The illusion is compromised by the artist's insecure grasp of perspective.

ABOVE The soft grays and browns, pastel greens, and pinks of this fresco at the Villa di Geggiano are central to the Italian palette and coordinated to the room's overall decor.

LEFT Tasseled valances and pleated drapes, characteristically worked in golden-yellow, make reference to Classical Roman porticos.

CY-PRÈS
Julia

CROWN EXPRESSIONS
Snowdrift · SD–8

PAINT MAGIC/
JOCASTA INNES
Dusk Mauve

FIRED EARTH/
PAINT PORTFOLIO
Ceiling Blue

JOHN OLIVER
Village Green

PAINT LIBRARY
Tarlatan

SANDERSON SPECTRUM
Pilgrim Brown · 47–23M

J.W. BOLLOM & CO. LTD
NATURAL COLOR SYSTEM
S 2030–Y20R

RALPH LAUREN PAINT
NEW ZEALAND COLLECTION
Timber Brown · NZ01D

BELOW Extensive use is made of marble throughout the Palacio Real de Aranjuez. Here, contrasting colored marble is employed in the dado panels and doorcase, the geometric-pattern floor, and the baseboards.

PALACIO REAL DE ARANJUEZ

STANDING IN AN OASIS of fertile land within the dry plains south of Madrid, the Palacio Real de Aranjuez was conceived in the mid-16th century as a springtime residence for the Spanish monarchy. Construction began in c.1563, but was subject to numerous interruptions and took over two centuries to complete – the last wing being finished in 1778. Given the duration of the project, the architecture of the palace inevitably accommodates a number of different styles that evolved during the period.

The vast, highly theatrical imperial staircase, for example, constructed from limestone and marble between 1743 and 1746 by the architect Giacomo Bonavia, is typical of the late Baroque style of northern Italy, while its magnificent wrought-iron and gilded bronze balustrade, designed by Francisco Barranco, is in Rococo style. However, these and similar diversities of taste do not generally detract from the overall architectural homogeneity of the palace, and indeed, the finished

building remains essentially true in both style and spirit to the conception of its original architect, Juan Bautista de Toledo. Comprising a main section of central patio layout with classical facades flanked by two large arcaded wings enclosing a French-style courtyard of honor, it is essentially a Classically inspired palace that has the informal character of a Renaissance *villa regia* because it was designed to be open to the surrounding gardens.

Not surprisingly, many of the palace's rooms have been remodeled and redecorated over the centuries. The Porcelain Room, completed in 1763 and lined with Capodimonte porcelain plaques displaying *chinoiserie* imagery, is in the Rococo style, while the equally exotic Arab Room, decorated 1848–50, is typical of mid-19th-century "Spanish-Victorian" Moorish taste. Yet, as with the palace's exterior, such diversities of style are subsumed within a general commitment to the Classical repertoire of ornament and decoration. This is evident not only in the

ABOVE Although the Throne Room was redecorated and partly refurnished in the mid-19th century, it retains a number of Neoclassical features from the reign of Charles IV (1788–1808) – a period during which it was used as a dining room. Most notable is the pair of Louis XVI-style giltwood *fauteuils* on the dais, which are upholstered in deep red velvet embroidered with gold wreaths. The combination of red velvet upholstery, wall panels, and tasseled canopy, with a "marble-green" *socle* and decorative gilding, is characteristic of Spanish Empire-style taste.

ABOVE The richness of color characteristic of Empire-style decoration is evident in this interior. A fine balance is struck between the warmer red tones of the chairs and wall hangings, and the cooler blue, black, and white of the baseboards and floor.

BELOW Here the strong tones of green, yellow, pink, brown, and blue in the wall hangings and textiles are enriched with a profusion of gilded ornament and relieved with the white grounds of the vaulted ceiling and dado paneling.

profile and configuration of the architectural moldings, and the geometric patterns of the marble floors, but also in the Classical motifs employed in the fabrics. The late 18th- and early 19th-century furniture and decorative artifacts such as clocks, vases, mirrors, chandeliers, and statuary are inspired in form and decoration by Classical examples, while the palace is hung with many paintings whose subject is derived from Greco-Roman mythology.

The wealth of Classically inspired architecture, ornament, and decoration at the Palacio Real de Aranjuez is not, however, confined to the principal structure. In one of its gardens stands the Real Casa del Labrador – a royal lodge built 1791–1803 and considered by many to be the Neoclassical jewel in the royal crown (see pp.88–91).

ABOVE Classical imagery recurs throughout this drawing room. Prominent motifs are the lion-paw feet of the giltwood-and-glass tripod table, the carved foliate C-scrolls on the backs of the armchairs, and the rectilinear moldings on the doors. Strong, saturated colors are used in the carpet, but the overall color scheme – dominated by pale blue and sepia, and pearlescent white – is lighter than that in the rooms seen above and below left.

REAL CASA DEL LABRADOR

LEFT Begun *c*.1801 and completed *c*.1808, the Platinum Room is a fine example of the luxurious Empire style. The room's finely figured mahogany *boiseries* are embellished with a sumptuous combination of painted grotesques and gilt-bronze and platinum motifs derived from Classical ornament. Classical motifs recur within the geometric pattern of the marble floor and on the chair (designed by the French furniture maker Jacob-Desmalter).

THE REAL CASA del Labrador ("Royal Laborer's House") was built as a royal lodge within the grounds of the Palacio Real de Aranjuez (see pp.86–7). Construction began in 1791, and under Juan de Villanueva and his assistant architects Antonio López Aguado and Isidro González Velázquez, the project was subject to two distinct architectural design phases prior to completion in 1803.

Initially, the two-story building (with an attic) was erected on a rectangular floor plan and its plain exterior faced with brick and stone. From 1799, two porticoed wings were added, enclosing a courtyard, and the exterior was embellished with Neoclassical ornament, including vaulted niches (with sculptures), garlands of flowers, and *putti*. Unfortunately, these additions were rather unsympathetically matched to the original structure, poorly constructed, and badly maintained, and they required major renovations during the 20th century. However, most of the interiors of the second phase have survived intact and, by contrast, are of exceptional quality.

Conceived mainly by the French decorator Jean-Démosthène Dugourc, all the interiors are Neoclassical. But, there are considerable diversities of style between the lodge's 19 rooms, each of which has its own character. The Sculpture Gallery, for example, with its marble and mosaic floor, Corinthian pilasters, vaulted niches, and Roman statuary, is designed in the late 18th-century style of Louis XVI.

In contrast, the Platinum Room, "sub-contracted" to Napoleon's decorators Charles Percier and Pierre Fontaine, is embellished with motifs derived from Etruscan, Imperial Roman, ancient Egyptian, and Renaissance ornament, and is a fine example of the more eclectic French Empire style that became fashionable in the early 19th century. That such nuances of Neoclassicism are almost seamlessly accommodated within one building and that decorations and furnishings of such visual richness do not overpower the rather small rooms is testament to a sure sense of coherent design that may have eluded the Casa del Labrador's architects, but certainly blessed its decorators.

RIGHT The Water Closet was modeled by the architect Isidro González Velázquez on designs drawn by the French decorator Jean-Démosthène Dugourc. The room's centerpiece is a throne modeled on ancient Roman marble prototypes. It is set in a niche lined with gilt-bronze Neoclassical motifs and panels of a brilliant blue, intricately figured Spanish marble.

ABOVE The walls of the overtly Neoclassical Sculpture Room are lined with niches and Corinthian pilasters made of plaster in imitation of marble. The figures and busts are mainly Roman copies of Greek originals.

ABOVE In Queen Maria Luisa's room (see pp. 90–1) a marble top console table by Dugourc stands in front of tapestry-woven wall hangings. The gilt-bronze early 19th-century clock depicts a Roman goddess and is flanked by a pair of candelabra incorporating winged figures, also from Classical antiquity.

"Dugourc was one of the principal designers in the transition from the Louis XVI style to the Empire style…"

(José Luis Sancho Gaspar, writer)

RIGHT The walls of Queen Maria Luisa's Room are lined with tapestry-woven hangings of sepia-tone silk, made in Lyons, France, that incorporate 93 views of locations in Spain and Italy. A firescreen with a Pompeiian-red, white, and gilt frame stands in front of the Carrara marble chimneypiece. The Empire-style stools and console tables around the perimeter of the room were designed by Jean-Demosthene Dugourc. The clock under the crystal chandelier is gilt-bronze, as is the griffin-legged table on which it stands. The pattern of the rug recalls the geometric- and floral-patterned marble floors of ancient Rome, and is laid over Spanish porcelain floor tiles.

Using the Spanish Neoclassical palette

French decorators such as Jean Dugourc, Charles Percier, and Pierre Fontaine were very influential in Spain, and thus there are strong similarities between the Spanish and French Neoclassical palettes (for the latter see pp.68–9). In the Spanish palette, favored paler colors for ceilings, plastered walls, and woodwork include white, sepia, and light gray and pink. Stronger hues, mostly used in wall hangings and textiles, include Pompeiian, crimson, and claret red; and aconite, Chinese, and lemon yellow. Other prominent colors include the lustrous brown tones of hardwood furniture, and gilding on moldings and artifacts.

LEFT Silk damask wall hangings, or wallpapers made in imitation of them, were often employed in the reception rooms of palaces and grander Spanish houses during the late 18th and early- to mid-19th centuries. Favored colors included various yellows, such as aconite, Chinese, and pale lemon.

BELOW Rich, saturated colors are characteristic of Spanish Empire-style textile furnishings. Here red damask *portières* frame double doors painted in stone colors.

ABOVE The imperial staircase at the Palacio Real de Aranjuez features a Rococo wrought-iron balustrade with gilt-bronze highlights. Its white and off-white color scheme is reminiscent of Classical Roman civic architecture.

RIGHT The warm rich tones of hardwood furniture, often augmented with gilt ornament and sometimes with ebonized details, feature strongly in late 18th- and 19th-century Spanish interiors.

LEFT Pinkish reds were also popular colors for silk wall hangings, wallpapers, and upholstery in early 19th-century Spanish interiors. Tones such as crimson- and claret-pink were thought to provide appropriate backgrounds for mahogany and rosewood furniture, and gilt and bronze artifacts.

RIGHT Pale gray, blue and sepia applied on white grounds were often used for Neoclassical grotesque wall paintings.

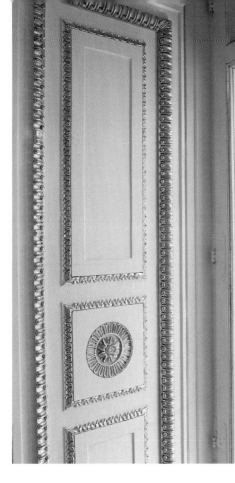

ABOVE Wooden fixtures and fittings are often painted a white or off-white hue similar to that of white Spanish limestone. Gilt highlights are also typical of Spanish Neoclassical style.

ABOVE RIGHT Classical and Egyptian imagery inspired the polychromatic painted ceilings of grander Spanish interiors during the early part of the 19th century.

RIGHT These red and gold giltwood *fauteuils* at the Palacio Real de Aranjuez show the influence of Napoleonic Empire style.

ABOVE The Sculpture Gallery in the Real Casa del Labrador is pure Spanish Neoclassical. The walls are plaster pigmented in imitation of marble; the columnar plinths for the statues are, like the floor, real marble.

LEFT The colors and motifs in the Billiard Room at the Real Casa del Labrador reveal the late 18th- and early 19th-century transition in Spain from Neoclassical Etruscan to Empire taste.

BOSCOBEL

LEFT Boscobel was constructed in 1804–7, in the Neoclassical Federal style. Its south facade features a double-height portico with square and round columns. The wooden window frames, door, and balustrades are picked out in white against the sandy yellow paint of the weather-boarded walls. Externally, Boscobel presents a restrained, distinctly American interpretation of Neoclassical architecture and ornament.

"…a delightful example of Federal domestic architecture." (Berry B. Tracy, art historian)

TODAY, BOSCOBEL stands on a bluff overlooking the river in Garrison-on-Hudson, New York. However, this fine example of Federal domestic architecture started life elsewhere, in Crugers, New York, on the site of the Franklin D. Roosevelt Veterans' Hospital. There the building was begun in 1804 as the dream house of one States Morris Dyckman, who planned his creation meticulously, but unfortunately did not live long enough to occupy it. Instead, his widow, Elizabeth Corne Dyckman, moved into the house in 1808 with her son Peter. It was the start of an improbable history for an elegant building that came into being at a time when Neoclassical architecture and decoration, already fashionable in Europe, was establishing firm roots on the east coast of the United States. Boscobel was to enshrine an American interpretation of the style, although the house's future frequently looked as ill-starred as that of the man whose dream it had been.

The house remained in the Dyckman family for 80 years, after which, in troubled circumstances, it passed out of their hands. By the early years of the 20th century, Boscobel faced the prospect of demolition – to the point where, in 1941, the United States government auctioned off the house as surplus property and accepted a bid of $35. However, a last-minute rescue operation followed,

RIGHT In the Entrance Hall, the main staircase rises from the central section of a triple arch of stylized Classical columns. The Brussels-weave stair runner with a green, tan, and red Venetian stripe pattern is a reproduction of the original carpet chosen by Mrs. Dyckman in May 1808.

LEFT Boscobel, originally built in Crugers, New York, was relocated to the Hudson highlands in 1951. The view from the house takes in West Point and the Hudson River as it cuts a gorge through the Appalachian Mountains.

LEFT The hall table is part of a Federal three-part mahogany dining table, made *c.*1800 in New York. The carved and gilded pier glass features *églomisé* panels, and was probably made by John Doggett in *c.*1800. The Federal-style rush-seated fancy chairs (from a set of 12 chairs and two settees) are painted green and gold, and date to *c.*1808.

RIGHT The wallpaper in the hall and on the stairs is a distinctive reproduction of an original of *c.*1804. The pale, stone-colored paint on the woodwork was also matched to original samples found in the mansion.

BELOW In the Front Drawing Room, the swagged-and-tailed valances are made from yellow-gold wool moreen and edged with pendant wooden spools wound with silk thread. The sheers, tied back on brass rosettes, are of embroidered white mull. The seats of the Federal mahogany chairs are attributed to Duncan Phyfe (*c*.1810), and are upholstered in a brighter yellow wool moreen trimmed with blue woven tape. The Wilton carpet has a blue, brown, and gold flower and ribbon pattern, and replaces the original carpet bought in 1808.

led by Benjamin Frazier of Garrison-on-Hudson. With the aid of benefactor Lila Acheson Wallace, he arranged for the house to be dismantled brick by brick and stored in barns and garages in and around the Garrison area. The present location in the nearby Hudson highlands was then found and Boscobel was gradually reassembled and reappointed. It was finally opened to the public in May 1961.

With its pillars and pediment, verandas, and tripartite Palladian motif windows, the two-story house presents a symmetrical Federal facade to the lush grounds into which it was transplanted. Its real riches, however, are to be found within. The restored architectural fixtures and fittings,

furniture, and textiles of Boscobel bear testimony to the thoughtful acquisitions of States Morris Dyckman, whom records show to have been very precise in his specifications and purchases. Dyckman's taste was sophisticated and cosmopolitan and, whether he was commissioning furniture from Europe or from the United States, his guiding principle was always the overall harmony of his creation – he did not adhere to the flag-waving Federalism that patriotically favored domestic products over those of the U.S.A.'s former colonial governors. Boscobel is today appointed to look like "new," as when the bereaved Mrs. Dyckman and her son first moved in.

ABOVE The windows in the Upstairs Sitting Room are covered with swagged valances and drapes made from English chintz, block-printed in Pompeiian red, yellow-gold, and black. The walls are flat-painted to echo the yellow-gold background of the fabric. The grass matting on the floor has a brown and white pattern.

FAR LEFT Peter Dyckman's room has a Federal mahogany bed, made *c*.1815 in New York and dressed with a white cotton dimity canopy and candlewick bedspread. The mahogany drop-leaf table is attributed to Duncan Phyfe; the cheval mirror to Charles Honoré Lannuier. The blue, brown, and white ingrain carpet dates to *c*.1820.

LEFT The swagged and pleated bed hangings in Mrs. Dyckman's room are of green silk moiré trimmed with red and green tassels; the bedspread is of green, white, and pink striped moiré.

ABOVE The pale orange-brown "Braintree" pattern wallpaper in Peter Dyckman's bedroom is a reproduction of the original 1807 paper; the reproduction border patterns are known as "Daisy" and "Portsmouth." The window drapes, like the bed hangings (see top left), are of white cotton dimity. The Federal mahogany "lolling" chair was made in New York *c*.1820 – its *curule*-style design is based on the chairs used by Roman magistrates. The Federal mahogany washstand, with enclosed basin, predates it by about ten years.

RIGHT The striped blue, gold, and green wallpaper in Elizabeth Dyckman's bedroom is a reproduction of the 1805 original. The George III trellis-pattern needlework carpet was made in England in the early 19th century. The tracery on the entablature of the fireplace, like its fluted columnar jambs, is a typical Regency design.

LEFT The Dining Room at the Morris–Jumel Mansion has been restored to its late 18th- and early 19th-century appearance. The wallpaper, with its vertical pattern of small, repeated motifs, is typical of the Neoclassical Federal style. The wooden fireplace is painted a late Colonial or early Federal blue (containing Prussian blue pigment).

ABOVE When Stephen and Eliza Jumel adopted their daughter Mary Bowen in the 1820s, this room became her bedchamber. The furniture is a little later, however – the four-poster bed dates to *c.*1840 and the "metamorphic" desk-and-chair unit to *c.*1850. The walls were recently repainted a medium green that resembles the color used during Mary's occupancy.

MORRIS–JUMEL MANSION

THE MORRIS–JUMEL MANSION has the distinction of being Manhattan's oldest surviving house. Sitting at the top of Harlem Heights between 160th and 162nd Streets, it has been through two major design phases: the first, grand late Colonial in style; the second, beginning in 1810, Neoclassical. The house was built in 1765 as a summer retreat for the British colonel Roger Morris and his American wife, Mary Philipse. At some 8,500 square feet (800 square meters), it was the centerpiece of a country estate, Mount Morris, then 11 miles (18 kilometers) from the center of the young New York City. The Georgian style of the house was very advanced for its time, bringing a particularly well-developed sense of Palladian harmony to both the facade and the interior.

Colonel Morris was the son of an English architect (also named Roger Morris) who was active in England during the first half of the 18th century and was a significant figure in the history of Palladianism; it seems likely that the influence of the older Morris was at work in the New York mansion. The original house design included a two-story portico and triangular pediment, classical columns, and a large octagonal room at the rear – the latter was the first of its kind to be seen in America. A number of external decorative effects also extended the range of conventional Colonial design: dentils at the tops of the walls encircled the house; doors were intricately carved; the wooden structure had its foundations disguised as brownstone; and the public face of the house was also disguised as stone with the aid of sand-textured paint. The rear, by contrast, was shingled, since it would only be seen by the servants. Inside, both the first and second floors were given spacious central halls, which served as reception and entertainment areas, and four rooms were disposed around the halls on each level. Below, a basement area served as the living and working quarters for servants, and also included a root cellar, wine cellar, dairy, and kitchen.

LEFT Taking full advantage of its elevated position on Harlem Heights, the Morris–Jumel Mansion boasts an elegant double-height portico with four Tuscan columns, two pilasters, and a dentilled triangular pediment. The facade is constucted from wood, but has been covered with off-white sand-textured paint so it resembles stone.

ABOVE The chambers at the Morris–Jumel Mansion used by George Washington in 1776 have been renovated in accordance with scientific paint analysis. The solid-colored reproduction wallpaper is verdigris green; the wooden fireplace, which has marble jambs and lintel, is painted warm gray to match the rest of the woodwork.

RIGHT The solid mid-green, white, and wood tones used in Mary Bowen's bedchamber of the 1820s is characteristic of the mansion's secondary bedrooms. The rather utilitarian style is reminiscent of many 18th-century Colonial rooms (see pp.36–53).

Colonel Morris's nationality, together with his house's location in a position that commanded views of downtown Manhattan, New Jersey, and Westchester, were to prove significant to subsequent developments. On the outbreak of the Revolutionary War, Morris left for England, and the house was occupied by, in turn, George Washington, the British Lieutenant-General Sir Henry Clinton, and the Hessian commander Baron Willhelm von Knyphausen. The martial theme of these tenancies was no accident: as a military vantage point, Morris's old retreat was unrivaled.

After the war, the mansion was confiscated by the American government, and for a time became Calumet Hall, a tavern on the Albany Post Road. Then, in 1810, it was bought by Stephen Jumel, a rich French merchant, and entered its second design phase. The front door was rebuilt "in the latest style"; stained glass was installed in both halls; and Jumel's wife, Eliza, completely refurbished many rooms in Empire style, bringing numerous fabrics and many pieces of furniture back with her from a trip to Paris.

In 1832, Stephen Jumel died, and his widow later married former Vice-President Aaron Burr in the mansion's front parlor. The marriage lasted six months. During her later years, Eliza Jumel was immensely wealthy, but she

ABOVE The front parlor of the Morris–Jumel Mansion is quintessential American Neoclassical of c.1830. The green wallpaper with foliate stripes is a reproduction of the original. The carpet has a classic Greek Revival pattern. The crystal chandelier is French and dates to c.1800. The saber-legged parlor set, embellished with gilt rosettes, belonged to Eliza Jumel. The Empire-style pier table and the circular, marble-topped table both date to c.1825; the latter is attributed to Joseph Meeks.

LEFT The bedchamber of former Vice-President Aaron Burr, Eliza Jumel's second husband, has been redecorated the way it would have appeared c.1833. The pale yellowish-green wallpaper has a delicate floral pattern, but most of the colors and patterns are richer than elsewhere in the house.

went into mental decline before her death in 1865. For almost 20 years, the Morris–Jumel estate remained in litigation. Eliza had come from a penniless Rhode Island family, and her *arriviste* attempts to blend in with New York society had failed dismally. Bad feelings had subsequently soured her relations with her surviving family, many of whom continued to live in the house after her death.

The property was in fact variously occupied for several years, at one time by a man who used it to demonstrate his "new" invention, the motion picture camera – a lawsuit from Thomas Edison resulted in his sudden disappearance. At the turn of the 20th century, the house was bought by its last private owners, Ferdinand and Lillie Earle, who recognized its historical importance. On Ferdinand's death, Lillie encouraged the city to buy the estate, and three local chapters of the Daughters of the American Revolution opened the mansion as a museum in 1907. Twelve of the period rooms are now restored, including the octagonal drawing room, a dining room, and Eliza's bedchamber.

ABOVE Eliza Jumel's bedchamber was decorated in the French Empire style. The walls are covered with a bright green paper, and divided into frieze, field, and dado by paper cutouts displaying Classical motifs. The colors of the French geometric-pattern carpet echo those of the wallpapers and fabrics. Napoleon Bonaparte supposedly once owned the *lit-en-bateau*.

LEFT In the Hall, which also served as a receiving room, a more restrained color scheme is employed. As above, the classic tripartite division of the walls is achieved using paper cutouts. The Empire-style pier table and mirror glass are American and date to *c.*1825.

OLD MERCHANT'S HOUSE

S EABURY TREDWELL was typical of the 19th-century New York merchants who commuted by horse-drawn omnibus from their townhouses to business at the South Street seaport. In 1835, he and his wife Eliza had moved their family of seven children into a red-brick and white-marble rowhouse – 29 East Fourth Street – in what was then known as the Bond Street area, an exclusive residential neighborhood east of Washington Square. The house had been built three years earlier, but the Tredwells made it their own; today, it is known as Old Merchant's House and reflects almost a century of their continuous occupancy. A living museum, it is modern New York City's only family home to have been preserved fully intact from the 19th century. Its contemporary ambience was that of nearby Washington Square, and the novelist Henry James described the Bond Street neighborhood as "…the most delectable. It has a kind of established repose…a riper, richer, more honorable look."

The exterior of Old Merchant's House presents a late-Federal facade, dormer windows, and a fanlight above the front door. Inside, the fine Greek Revival interiors include formal parlors featuring identical black and gold marble mantelpieces, an Ionic double-column screen, and mahogany pocket doors that separate the rooms. The matching plaster ceiling medallions are among the finest

ABOVE The swagged-and-tailed, heavily tasseled bed hangings in Seabury Tredwell's bedroom are made from rich scarlet wool damask. The mahogany bed, embellished with gilded floral ornament, dates to *c*.1835.

BELOW Mrs. Tredwell's bedroom is seen here dressed for summer: the bed hangings and window drapes are made from light cotton fabric; the floor covering is reproduction diamond-pattern "china matting."

that exist. When built, the house included all the modern technological conveniences of the era, including piping for gas lights, a 4,000-gallon (15,000-liter) cistern, and the latest bell system for summoning the servants. It also features some particularly fine furniture, including pieces from New York's foremost cabinetmakers – most notably Duncan Phyfe and Joseph Meeks – together with numerous opulent fabric furnishings and decorative artifacts.

Over the years, as New York City continued to grow, the Tredwells' neighbors gradually abandoned the district for more elegant houses farther uptown. The Tredwells remained on East Fourth Street, however. Gertrude, the eighth and last Tredwell child, who was born soon after the family moved in, never married and continued to live in the house until she died in an upstairs bedroom in 1933 at the age of 92. Three years later, the house was opened as a museum. Today, this original, late-Federal classic can fairly claim a greater degree of period authenticity than most restored and refurbished house-museums.

Left Standing on lion's paw feet and embellished with carved eagles and brass rosettes, this Empire-style mahogany *chaise longue* and bolster is upholstered with a reproduction floral-pattern red silk damask.

Above The carpet in the Greek Revival double parlor is a reproduction of the 19th-century original. Its bold geometric pattern, rendered in red, yellow, and blue on an off-white ground, is characteristic of the period.

Left The architectural conceit of a mirror-image double parlor perfectly embodies the fundamental symmetry of the Greek Revival style. The division between the parlors is marked by two pairs of Ionic columns, with sliding pocket doors between. As in many other rooms, off-white walls, columns, and ceiling provide a classic, neutral backdrop that enhances the richer colors of the fabrics, furniture, and artefacts such as the gilt pier glass.

Above Neoclassical motifs, such as dentil and egg-and-dart moldings and rectilinear door panels, dominate the fixtures and fittings. Concessions are also made to other styles, as the Rococo-Revival gasolier (gas chandelier) bears witness.

Using the American Neoclassical palette

During the early years of the Federal period (1780–1850), Colonial color schemes (see pp.36–53) remained fashionable in the United States, especially in rural areas. They were gradually superseded, however, by a brighter, lighter palette inspired by contemporary European models. Favored wall colors included pale terracottas; straw, citron, and Chinese yellows; pale blues and greens; and a range of grayish and other off-white stone colors – the latter were also often used on wooden moldings and were particularly prevalent on all surfaces in Greek Revival interiors. More saturated, richer tones of red, yellow, and blue were also employed, notably in Empire-style rooms. However, these tended to be confined to upholstery, and to draperies, carpets, and other floor coverings patterned with Neoclassical and plant-form motifs.

RIGHT This handblocked wallpaper, simulating ashlar masonry in "natural" stone colors, is typical of the *trompe l'oeil* papers that were fashionable in early 19th-century Federal houses.

BELOW Grayish-green and yellowish-green wall finishes were popular. The colors were often enlivened with gilding, as in this Federal carved *girandole* (convex) mirror.

ABOVE Yellow wall finishes were also in vogue in Neoclassical interiors and, as here, were often painted to match the fabric furnishings. The white cotton drapes at the windows contribute to the lightness of the room.

MIDDLE LEFT Vertical stripe-pattern wallpapers were also particularly popular in Neoclassical interiors on both sides of the Atlantic.

LEFT The grandest chimneypieces were made of stone or marble, but wooden fireplaces (as shown here), painted white or a stone color, were more common.

ABOVE White or off-white walls are particularly prevalent in Greek Revival interiors. Here, they are boldly contrasted with the rich red tones of the upholstery and window drapes, and the lustrous reddish-brown patina of the mahogany door.

RIGHT Panels of a darker-colored wallpaper are used in this parlor. However, the characteristic lightness of the decorative scheme is maintained by the off-white and stone colors on the painted woodwork and by the pearl-white upholstery.

ABOVE This combination of mid-green and white dates to *c*.1820 and demonstrates the lingering influence in the early 19th century of the 18th-century Colonial palette (see pp.36–53). Such color schemes were usually confined to secondary bedrooms in grander Neoclassical houses.

RIGHT Toward the end of the Neoclassical period of American architecture and interior design, richer colors and more convoluted patterns became fashionable, heralding the emergence of the heavier style of High Victorian decoration (see pp.116–29).

J.W. BOLLOM & CO. LTD
NATURAL COLOR SYSTEM
S 2005–Y60R

SANDERSON SPECTRUM
Kittiwake Grey • 47–17M

OLD VILLAGE PAINTS
WILLIAMSBURG
3–6 Fancy Chair Yellow

CROWN EXPRESSIONS
Mustard Spice • MS–9

RALPH LAUREN PAINTS
SOUTHPORT COLLECTION
Driving Cap • SO04C

PAINT LIBRARY
Very Well Read

ACE ILLUMINATIONS
Warren Woods • 154–A

THE OLD FASHIONED
MILK PAINT CO., INC.
Federal Blue

FARROW & BALL
Sugar Bag Light • U/C22

SÖRBY MANOR HOUSE

RIGHT The reproduction Gustavian settee designed by Sörby's owner, Lars Sjöberg, is upholstered with a documentary fabric that displays a bold *chinoiserie* plant-form pattern indicative of the influence of Chinese decoration in Sweden in the late 18th century. As in many other rooms in the house, the floorboards are pickled, their grayish-white hue echoed in the ground color of the walls.

BELOW The painted panels on the field of the wall in the sitting room (see right) are embellished with swags and tails of flowers and leaves. The high quality of the painting, in which subtle color gradations give the motifs a naturalistic, three-dimensional quality, is typical of Swedish Neoclassical decoration.

THE SÖRBY MANOR HOUSE, near Mosäs in Sweden, is owned by Lars Sjöberg, a designer and international authority on Swedish architecture and decoration. The house was built in the 1660s and partly remodeled in the 1760s. One of the most significant modifications was the insertion of additional windows, which has had the effect of substantially lightening the interior. The walls are made from squared, de-barked logs – a traditional method of wall-construction in a country with substantial timber resources and one that provided very effective insulation against the harshness of Scandinavian winters. For much of the 20th century, the outside of the house was painted white, but in the 1990s it was repainted the original iron-oxide red. This color, together with ocher, is typical of the houses and barns of the region and was also popular in 18th-century Colonial America (see pp.36–53), where there was an influx of Scandinavian immigrants.

From a decorative point of view, however, it is the interior of the Sörby manor house that is most interesting. Indeed, although distressed by natural wear and tear over the passage of time, the painted decorations that have survived from the 1780s provide an excellent insight into many of the core elements of the Neoclassical Gustavian style that gradually superseded the Swedish Rococo style (see pp.54–9) during the last quarter of the 18th century.

Of particular note are the interior paneled walls, which in the principal rooms display the Classical tripartite division of frieze, field, and dado – in this case, the narrow frieze surmounting a field and dado of almost equal depth. As in many other Swedish houses of the period, the divisions between the three sections are primarily delineated by painted *trompe l'oeil* rather than architectural moldings of plaster or wood. Also characteristic, especially of Gustavian-style decoration in rural areas, is the further

ABOVE Cobalt blue has been a popular color in Sweden since the Middle Ages and is the predominant hue seen in the flower and leaf motifs at Sörby. The pigment used for the rectilinear borders around this example is iron-oxide red.

BELOW The Classical division of walls into frieze, field, and dado is achieved at Sörby, as in many Swedish houses, with painted *trompe l'oeil* effects and contrasts of color rather than with wooden or plaster molding or wallpaper.

division of the fields into rectilinear panels, comprising iron-oxide red lines on a chalky gray-white ground, embellished with either interlaced floral motifs or Neoclassical swags. These motifs are hand-painted with egg tempera in shades of cobalt blue, iron-oxide red, and white.

Although the house is sparsely furnished, everything is quintessentially Gustavian. Notable pieces include a rustic ladderback chair with a cobalt-blue finish; an off-white-painted spindle-back chair reproduced by Lars Sjöberg from an original 1780–90 "Sörby" chair found in the house (now on loan to a museum); and a white-painted reproduction Gustavian settee, upholstered with a documentary blue and white floral-patterned fabric, which was designed by Sjöberg for the home-furnishing company Ikea's Gustavian line. The commercial success of the latter testifies to the popularity in the late 20th and early 21st centuries of this understated, elegant style.

ABOVE The late 20th- and early 21st-century revival of interest in Gustavian style is partly fueled by its decorative palette – the combination of strong cobalt blue and cool grayish white, in particular, appeals to a Post-Modern aesthetic. Equally resonant are the rectilinear and relatively unornamented forms of Gustavian painted furniture. The design of the original rustic Gustavian chair above, like that of the more polite reproduction Gustavian chair shown left, dates to the late 18th century, but could just as easily have been conceived in the late 20th century.

JULITA MANOR HOUSE

THE JULITA MANOR HOUSE and estate is located in Södermanland, a province 100 miles (160 kilometers) west of Stockholm. During the Middle Ages, the site was occupied by a wealthy Cistercian monastery that was a place of pilgrimage and a thriving center of cultural, social, and agricultural development. In the early 16th century, the monastery was confiscated by King Gustav Vasa, who was intent on making Sweden a Lutheran rather than a Catholic country. The monks fled and, aided by a loan from the Crown, the first of a number of private owners took over the estate. In 1745, the original manor house was destroyed in a fire and was replaced with the building (completed in 1760) that survives to this day. In 1941, the house was donated to Sweden's Nordic Museum.

A number of historical, architectural, and decorative styles are represented at the house. For example, it has two adjacent wings in the late Swedish Baroque style; there are several interiors and displays representing feudal peasant life; and a smoking room is decorated and furnished with the rich colors and densely grouped furniture characteristic of late 19th-century Swedish-Victorian style. However, most of the principal rooms are decorated and furnished in the Neoclassical Gustavian style that superseded Swedish Rococo during the late 18th and early 19th centuries and enjoyed a revival during the early 20th century.

The inspiration for these Gustavian interiors is primarily French Neoclassicism (see pp.64–9), with echoes of the Rococo style in some pieces of furniture and with elements of traditional Chinese imagery accommodated in some of the fabrics and wallpapers. All of these styles, however, have been rendered uniquely Swedish in the Julita Manor House by the use of a palette of pale colors – such as light yellow, gray and blue – that is distinctively Gustavian. They are often subtly enlivened with gilding.

BELOW Known as the Blue Room because of the blue ground of its Neoclassical wallpaper panels (also see right) and its pale blue and white striped upholstery, this salon is furnished as it was *c.*1800. The set of white-painted furniture is made in the Neoclassical Directoire style that flourished in France during the last five years of the 18th century. Sparsely ornamented and rather austere, the style is consonant in form and spirit with the Swedish Gustavian style. The set's two x-frame stools with lions'-paw feet are modeled on Classical Greek prototypes known as *diphros okladias.*

LEFT The wallpaper in the Blue Room is a typical Neoclassical design, combining bands of delicately spiraling floral motifs with urns, mythological and human figures, and *trompe l'oeil* architectural moldings from Classical antiquity.

RIGHT Since the 18th century, the dining room walls and doors have been repainted many times in the original cool grayish tone that is one of the core colors of the Gustavian palette. The wall painting above the door, like others in the room, was done in the 1760s. The Rococo-style chairs were made in the early 20th century by estate carpenter Henning Forsman.

BELOW In one of the bedrooms, the wallpaper and *toile* window drapes, bed hangings, and bed panels are patterned with blossom and other plant-form imagery inspired by traditional Chinese decoration. They are rendered in the Gustavian colors of very pale straw yellow and pale grayish-blue.

"Straw yellows, cool greys and muted blues are typically Gustavian." (Jenny Gibbs, writer)

ABOVE The Gustavian-style Balcony Room is an extension that was built as a summer dining room in the early 20th century by Arthur Bäckström, the last private owner of the house.

A GUSTAVIAN-STYLE FARMHOUSE

LEFT The study is a rectilinear composition, in which the pairs of wall-mounted plate racks and tables flanking the fireplace impose a formal discipline on a room that still manages to have a lighthearted effect. This is primarily achieved by contrasting the white ceilings and furniture with a "French lilac" shade on the flat-plastered walls. The effect is enhanced by the Neoclassical festoon motif on the chimneypiece which, like the baseboard moldings, is highlighted in burnished Dutch metal "gold leaf". A warmer note is struck by the dark-stained, butt-jointed floorboards. The preserving jars on the mantel and desktop filing cabinet contain fabric swatches (see below) dyed to match the rest of the decor.

CREATIVE AND KNOWLEDGEABLE pastiches of historical decorative styles are sometimes just as revealing as slavish copies of them. A good example of this is the Swedish designer Lena Proudlock's recent redecoration and furnishing of her farmhouse in southwestern England, in which she has captured the essence of Swedish Gustavian Neoclassical decor.

Located near Tetbury in the Gloucestershire countryside, the farmhouse was built in 1784, and an extension was added at the back in 1804. When Lena Proudlock first viewed the property, its plain stone facade instantly suggested to her a practical, uncomplicated home that chimed with her personal aspirations at a time when she was seeking to divest herself of encumbrances on all fronts. The simplicity of the internal layout mirrored that of the exterior, and, apart from the removal of a flight of stairs to enlarge the kitchen and the addition of some new stairs to gain access to rooms beneath the roof, few major structural alterations were required.

On this spatial "clean slate," Lena Proudlock developed a decorative scheme in which neither the restrained, understated elegance of the Swedish Gustavian style, nor her own highly personal perspective on it, are ever compromised. Color – and, especially, a firm grasp of the Swedish Neoclassical palette of muted gray, green, lilac, mauve and white – was the key to her success.

An existing teak garden chair provided the inspiration for a pair of slatted wooden armchairs that now flank the fireplace in the living room. A sofa covered in black denim and a long trestle table represent the room's only other furniture – a degree of minimalism underscored by the graded shades of white with which the ceiling, walls, woodwork, and floor are painted. The first recognizable Neoclassical elements are the simple rectilinear moldings on the shutters, doors, and fireplace, all of which are burnished in Dutch-metal "gold leaf." Such gilding reappears in other rooms – not in the bold, commanding role it has so often assumed in more southerly European

ABOVE Swatches of colored fabrics convey a message in a bottle: color is an invaluable ingredient of decoration, to be used with panache – as Lena Proudlock says – in the way a top chef uses spices and herbs.

ABOVE Flowers and fallen petals
are a recurring decorative motif
in Lena Proudlock's home. Like
the family photographs hanging
on pegs in her bedroom
(see p.113), they add something
transitory, a touch of *memento
mori* to the solid geometric lines
of Neoclassical pastiche.

LEFT The farmhouse's original
18th-century stone floor survives
in the entrance hall, the walls of
which are painted "old white."
On the near side of the door, lilac
walls provide the backdrop for an
armchair slip-covered with a red
and white striped fabric. Striped
fabrics were fashionable in
Neoclassical interiors in France,
Sweden, and England.

LEFT Reproduction Gustavian chairs, their seats upholstered in blue denim, flank the table in the attic dining room. The bas-relief on the chimney breast depicts a figure with a lyre from Classical antiquity. The forged-iron chandelier adds a baronial touch to a small room that has been elegantly transformed into a light and airy dining area by the combination of light blue and white paints.

ABOVE In the kitchen, what was once convenient storage is transformed into an altar to style. The hutch's door-panel moldings are picked out in gold against a light blue ground. Most of the plates and tureens on display are Wedgwood's "Indian pheasant" pattern. The floorboards have been painted dove white, simulating the pickled wooden floors often found in 18th-century Swedish houses – the primary purpose of the pickling being to protect against insect infestation.

interiors, but as a restrained, recurring *leitmotif* applied to everything from dado rails and baseboards to stair panels and mirror frames. The dining room, in particular, manages effortlessly to suggest something of the "Nordic style" that Lena Proudlock once marketed in one of her businesses. Its white-painted wooden beams, chairs, bench, and tables – the latter with ice-blue tops – reflect Scandinavian vernacular elements transported from their familiar natural wood tones by applied color.

Above all, the whites and grays that suffuse the house further open up its internal spaces. The occasional calculated incongruity, such as bolts of pastel-colored denim stacked in a corner of her bedroom, seem part of an inclusive design approach, rather than the result of any Post-Modern inclination to play games. Such details, like the house in general, echo the essential spirit of Gustavian Neoclassicism, which took a French style and adapted it to its own aesthetic and cultural agenda.

BELOW Although pared down to a more minimalist modern aesthetic, the decorations and furnishings in this bedroom embody many of the core elements of Swedish Neoclassicism and are combined to recreate the understated elegance and austerity of ornament that characterized the Gustavian style. For example, the Swedish palette is represented in the gray-blue walls and the "dove white" painted woodwork. The four-poster bed is suitably rectilinear in form, as is the slatted bench by the footboard. The bed's fabric canopy, made from old ticking, has a favorite Neoclassical pattern of blue and white stripes. Likewise, the more colorful stylized floral motifs on the bedcover – in pinkish red, pale blue, and straw yellow – are also configured within an overall geometric pattern.

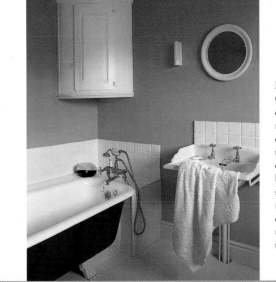

LEFT In this bathroom, Gustavian gray-blue walls are contrasted with a white sink, mirror, wall-hung corner cabinet, and floor and wall tiles; the sides of the white enameled cast-iron, roll-top bathtub are painted black. The shape of the curved cabinet recalls the large, columnlike ceramic stoves that were often used in Swedish houses during the 18th and 19th centuries.

RIGHT Lena Proudlock makes no distinction between her work as a fabric designer and her home life. Many of the farmhouse's painted tables, benches, and chairs are her own designs. Here, bolts of fabric from her collection of pastel denims are stored in a bedroom, where, against neutral colored walls, they become a decorative feature in their own right.

"Use color with panache, as a good cook uses herbs and spices."

(Lena Proudlock, owner of the house)

ABOVE In Lena Proudlock's bedroom, family photographs suspended from black-painted clothespins are displayed against the white-painted walls – a contemporary twist on the late 18th- and early 19th-century "print room," in which rows of prints and engravings were used to decorate walls. Her bed is painted cast iron, with brass finials on the corner posts.

Using the Swedish Neoclassical palette

The Gustavian palette is dominated by light hues, notably chalky off-white, pale blue, green, pink, and gray (*perl grot*) and straw yellow. They are primarily used as ground colors on walls, ceilings, and furniture painted to match; the off-whites are also evident in floorboards pickled to protect against infestations of insects. Stronger, richer colors, such as cobalt blue, cobalt green, and iron-oxide red, are mostly confined to hand-painted decorative motifs; to wooden, plaster, and *trompe l'oeil* architectural moldings; and to furniture and fabric patterns. Gilding, sometimes substituted with gold paint, is also used to highlight moldings.

LEFT Pale gray, chalky off-white, and burnished gold combine in this grand gallery and music room. The contrast between the gray and white ground colors helps define the architectural proportions of the room. The picture frame, wooden fillets framing the wall panels, and the Neoclassical motifs on the ceiling and pilasters are highlighted with gilding. The matte yellow-gold of the flat-painted wall panels and the fabric valances above the windows coordinates with the color scheme.

ABOVE Applied on a grayish-white ground, this flower-and-leaf motif is rendered in shades of cobalt blue and gray. It is interlaced around the edge of a simple rectilinear wall panel, the perimeter of which is painted a tint of iron-oxide red.

RIGHT The yellows in this Neoclassical cartouche depicting a figure beneath an arbor echo those of the gilded mantel mirror frame and the seat pads of the chairs.

ABOVE Gilding is used to pick out the Neoclassical motifs on this early 20th-century reproduction Gustavian armchair. The colors in the patterned ceramic tiles on the columnar Swedish heater behind it include a typically Gustavian coppery blue-green hue.

LEFT Numerous gradations of gray were used in Gustavian interiors. The gray paint on this wall and paneled door has a subtle green cast.

ABOVE LEFT The blue and white check fabric covering the seat pads of these reproduction Gustavian chairs was a popular choice in Swedish Neoclassical interiors.

ABOVE RIGHT The soft powdery bloom of these blue distemper paints is due to large quantities of chalk in the mix.

RIGHT During the 19th century, the lighter hues of the Gustavian palette were gradually ousted by the darker colors of the Swedish Victorian palette.

LEFT As part of a sympathetic late 20th-century pastiche of Swedish Gustavian style, "old white" latex paint on the walls is subtly contrasted with "dove white" latex on the floorboards – the latter applied to simulate a pickled finish.

RIGHT Swedish tiles were mainly tin- rather than lead-glazed and inspired by Dutch Delft designs, as on this tile stove with blue and white floral motifs.

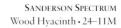

DULUX COLOUR SELECTOR
Tranquil Stone

SANDERSON SPECTRUM
Silver Wing · 44–7P

CROWN COLOUR PLANNER
Orchard Green

CROWN EXPRESSIONS
Misty Rose

ACE ILLUMINATIONS
Floral City · 134–B

**PAINT MAGIC/
JOCASTA INNES**
Dining Room Red

**PAINT MAGIC/
JOCASTA INNES**
Midnight

**RALPH LAUREN PAINT
COUNTRY CLUB COLLECTION**
Rowboat · CO01B

SANDERSON SPECTRUM
Wood Hyacinth · 24–11M

Victorian style

LEFT The Victorian Gothic Revival style was popular from the 1840s on. In Britain, houses often incorporated bands of Gothic-style polychrome masonry. In the United States, where lumber was more abundant, board-and-batten sidings were common. As at Roseland Cottage – built in Woodstock, Connecticut, in 1846 and now repainted its original pink with purple highlights – this usually resulted in a more colorful exterior decoration.

ABOVE Victorian stylistic eclectism is well represented in the library at the Mark Twain House in Hartford, Connecticut, decorated in 1881. Gold-on-turquoise wallpaper in *Japonaiserie* style contrasts with bookcase carvings – scrolling volutes flanking a demi-rosette – derived from the Classical orders.

ARCHITECTURE AND DECORATION during the Victorian era, which began in the late 1830s and continued until the beginning of the 20th century, was highly eclectic. Numerous styles became fashionable at different periods, many of them revivals and adaptations of earlier stylistic movements. Notable examples include the Gothic Revival, based on the architecture and ornament of medieval Europe; the Renaissance, Baroque, and Rococo Revivals; and various reincarnations of late 18th- and early 19th-century Neoclassical styles, including Adam, Empire, Regency, and Italianate – the last of these American and loosely based on the English Regency model. In addition, a major increase in international travel and trade resulted in further assimilation of Chinese, Japanese, Indian, Persian, and Arabian styles of ornament and decoration – collectively referred to in the West as "Oriental."

The era's stylistic eclectism manifested itself in a number of ways. Many houses were designed and decorated in one particular style, but in others different styles were allotted to specific rooms – a Gothic Revival library, for example, might be combined with a Rococo Revival bedroom, a Neoclassical entrance hall, and a Persian smoking room. It was also common practice to combine elements of the diverse styles within one elaborately decorated, densely furnished room. For adherents of the Arts and Crafts Movement, which emerged in the late 1860s, this amounted to little more than stylistic "clutter." They advocated instead a return to the simpler forms and higher standards of craftsmanship found in medieval vernacular dwellings, albeit enriched with Renaissance and Oriental motifs and imagery. Developed on both sides of the Atlantic up until World War II, this more coherent, "honest" style also helped to lay the ground for the rigorously rational approach of the Modernists.

ABOVE In the double parlor at Roseland Cottage, Gothic Revival forms and motifs include the pointed arch between the rooms (made of pine, but woodgrained to simulate oak); the pierced fretwork, pinnacles and crockets on the chair backs; and medieval-style, polychrome stained-glass windows.

LEFT Christophe Gollut's recent redecoration of an 1890s south London Victorian villa uses the lighter, less cluttered style that became fashionable in the latter part of the 19th century. The unobtrusive color scheme contrasts white flat-plaster ceilings with pale yellow walls, window frames, and balusters, and pale brown handrails and newel posts. More vibrant colors are restricted to the bands of stained glass in the late Victorian hanging light fixture.

ABOVE Vibrant yellow walls in a bedroom at Fred Hughes's townhouse, built in New York in 1889, recall the strong, saturated colors of early 19th-century Empire style. The furniture and artifacts are suitably eclectic, ranging from photographs of Native Americans to a Victorian ebonized traveling desk.

ROSELAND COTTAGE

ACQUIRED IN 1970 by the Society for the Preservation of New England Antiquities and subsequently designated a National Historic Landmark, Roseland Cottage was designed in 1846 by the English-born architect Joseph C. Wells as a summer residence for the wealthy businessman and influential Republican Party supporter Henry C. Bowen. The cottage, which is surrounded by several outbuildings including a barn and an icehouse, stands on a prominent hilltop location in Woodstock, Connecticut. It is built in the picturesque Victorian Gothic Revival style, a style initially popularized in the USA via the publications of the influential architectural writer Andrew Jackson Downing, who praised it for its "originality, boldness and energy," which made it "…ideally suited to the man of independent spirit."

With its steeply pitched, finialed gable roofs; its ornamental foliated crestings; its combination of lancet, dormer, and oriel windows using clear and stained leaded glass; and its emphasis on the perpendicular, the exterior of Roseland Cottage is characteristically Gothic Revival. The use of wooden board-and-batten sidings – here painted bright pink, an appropriate color for this romantic style of domestic Victorian architecture – is typically American.

In addition to the leaded windows with their diamond panes, the interior of the cottage also features a number of Gothic-style architectural fixtures and fittings, the most notable being a wooden lancet arch connecting the two halves of the double parlor. Likewise, much of the furniture is Gothic Revival, especially the upholstered chairs and

LEFT In the double parlor the Lincrusta frieze above the picture rail was applied in the 1880s. Lincrusta – linseed oil, gum, and wood pulp spread on canvas and embossed with patterns – was a popular wall covering in the late Victorian era.

RIGHT The wallpaper on the field below the Lincrusta is a typical example of the formalized leaf-pattern papers, rendered in naturalistic shades of green and pale brown, that were popular in late Victorian interiors.

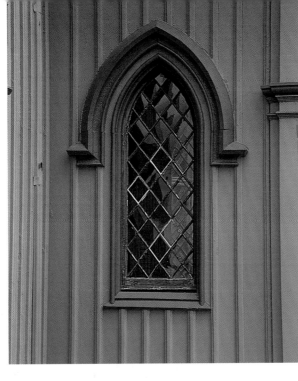

RIGHT & BELOW The board-and-batten sidings of Roseland Cottage have been repainted in the bright pink used in the 1880s. Gothic Revival features such as lancet windows and crestings are picked out in purple.

settees with lancet- or ogee-arched and pinnacled backs. Equally characteristic of the style is the interior color scheme, dominated by a range of brown, green, and yellow hues, seen in the patterned wallpapers and Lincrusta friezes, the mahogany and oak furniture, the painted doors and window frames and the stained and polished wooden floors. These comparatively muted tones, which include "ecclesiastical" dark browns redolent of the wooden fixtures and furniture found in the Gothic churches of medieval Europe, are enlivened by splashes of brighter color – most evident in red and blue upholstery, the blues and pinks of Oriental rugs, and the naturally illuminated reds, yellows, and greens of the stained glass.

RIGHT The shades of yellow and brown in the double parlor's wallpapers (see also opposite) are echoed in the Gothic Revival mahogany furniture, in the stained and polished butt-jointed floorboards and in the painted doors and baseboards. Injections of bolder color, characteristic of Victorian Gothic interiors, appear in the upholstery, the rugs, and more subtly, in the cornice and frieze, where the moldings are picked out in tones of gold, green, and pale and bright blues.

ABOVE Leaded polychrome stained-glass windows were often employed in Gothic Revival houses and made a significant contribution to interior color schemes. The yellow, red, and green panes in this window bay at Roseland Cottage imitate traditional diamond patterns. The mahogany-frame settee, upholstered in red plush with an ogee-arched and pinnacle-topped fretwork back, is a quintessential piece of American Gothic Revival furniture.

MARK TWAIN'S HOUSE

IN 1873, SAMUEL L. CLEMENS, better known as the writer Mark Twain, purchased the land for a house in an area known as Nook Farm on the outskirts of Hartford, Connecticut. The building, completed in 1874, was designed by the New York architect Edward Tuckerman Potter (1831–1904). Like many American Victorian homes of this period, it is architecturally eclectic. It combines Queen Anne-style patterned brickwork with features in the Stick style (see Glossary) including steeply gabled roofs, and verandas and porches with elaborate wooden balustrades.

The main rooms in the house were redecorated and refurnished in 1881 by Associated Artists, a prestigious group of interior decorators whose principal members included Louis Comfort Tiffany, Lockwood de Forest, Candace Thurber Wheeler, and Samuel Colman.

LEFT Vermilion and black paints are employed to accentuate the decorative configurations of the red brickwork at Mark Twain's House. Vermilion is also the color of the painted woodwork, and of some roof tiles – the latter contrasted with slate-gray tiles to create a subtle "diaper" pattern.

BELOW Wall and ceiling papers in the library feature a gold geometric stencil pattern on a turquoise-colored ground. The gold recurs in the gilded cornice and in numerous picture frames.

Throughout, their work is characterized by a subtle and harmonious use of color – red and pink, metallic gold and silver, blue and green, and the lustrous tones of polished wooden furniture. The inspiration for many of these colors, and for the stenciled patterns and motifs applied to flat plaster, wallpapers, and wooden dados in the principal rooms, was largely derived from non-Western sources. The interior of the Mark Twain House encapsulates the late 19th-century fashion for using African, Middle Eastern, Indian, Chinese, Japanese, and Native American colors and designs within a traditional European-based vocabulary of architecture, decoration, and ornament.

BELOW The dining room walls were refinished in 1881 with an embossed paper stenciled with a red and gold lily pattern. In the Victorian era, red was felt to be a particularly suitable background color for the display of gilt-framed paintings. The claret-red drape is plush velvet and is one of a pair of *portières* that divides the dining room and library.

"All interiors were ugly compared with the perfect taste of this ground floor, and its delicious dream of harmonious color." (Mark Twain, writer)

ABOVE The silver stenciled patterns on the wall paneling of the entrance hall, like the blue stenciled patterns on the Indian-red painted walls and ceilings, resemble Native American textiles and were probably designed by Tiffany. The hall chair is upholstered in a red floral-patterned damask.

LEFT The drawing-room walls are divided into a series of panels displaying East Indian-style patterns and motifs stenciled in silver on a salmon-pink ground. The design is attributed to Lockwood de Forest, who was well versed in the traditional art of Egypt, Syria, and India.

LEFT & ABOVE In a guest bedroom, the walls, doors, door and window frames, and baseboards have been uniformly painted a vivid tone of gloss-finish blue. The gold stars (a popular American motif) and stylized Classical-style leaf borders were stenciled in gold, which was then carried over to match the cornice. The pale yellow canopies fringed with red tassels that drape the four-poster mahogany beds (which date from *c*.1800) were made from drapes.

A HOUSE ON LEXINGTON AVENUE

FRED HUGHES WAS Andy Warhol's business manager, and bought his client's late Victorian four-story townhouse on Lexington Avenue, New York City, in the early 1970s. He subsequently restored the interior architecture of the house to its original state when built in 1889 by Henry J. Hardenbergh (architect of the Dakota, the first prestigious apartment block on Central Park).

The redecoration of the rooms – especially the use of strong, rich wall colors, such as emerald green, vivid blue, deep purple, and yellow-ocher – is typically High Victorian. As in the 19th century, these colors are further enriched by gilded moldings, stenciled motifs, and gilt picture frames. Lighter wall tones are also in evidence, notably pale yellow ivory and the "greige" (a mixture of gray and beige) used in the study. These are also authentic to the period, when they were primarily employed in bedrooms.

It is the furnishing of the house, however, that is most characteristically High Victorian. During the second half of the 19th century, it became increasingly fashionable to collect furniture from earlier eras, and Fred Hughes's magnificent collection follows in that tradition. Fine-quality European and American antiques – Adam, Empire, Regency, Federal, and Gothic Revival – are crammed into the principal rooms in true High Victorian style, the lustrous patina of their finely figured hardwoods, such as rosewood and mahogany, also making a major contribution to the decorative palette. Completing the picture, and confirming the High Victorian passion for diversity of style and ornament, are the eclectic displays of art and numerous *objets d'art* – ranging from 17th-century oils, statues by Canova, and late Georgian sconces to printed serigraphs by Warhol and Native American masks from Santa Fe.

RIGHT The fireplace in the emerald-green front living room (see also far right) has a *faux marbre* finish. Painted marble finishes were often applied to wooden and cast-iron chimneypieces during the Victorian era. Equally popular, and seen here on the overmantel mirror, were painted simulations of exotically grained and figured hardwoods such as rosewood, flame-cut mahogany, and heartgrain cuts of oak. As in most Victorian rooms, the mantel shelf here is used to display diverse artifacts.

ABOVE The fireplace and walls in Fred Hughes's study are painted in his favorite color: "greige." A mixture of gray and beige, this cool hue provides an unobtrusive neutral-colored background for displays of diverse paintings and *objets d'art*, and was much favored by the influential 20th-century American decorator Nancy Lancaster. Prominent among the artifacts on the mantel shelf are yellow, black, and white Zuni Pueblo masks from New Mexico.

RIGHT The walls and molding in the front living room are vivid emerald green. A more muted green appears in the upholstery fabrics. Apart from gold – in the picture frames, shell sconces, and molding below the cornice – the other prominent hues are the reds and reddish-browns in the center portrait and the rosewood frame of the 19th-century Russian sofa.

A LATE VICTORIAN LONDON VILLA

THIS SPACIOUS, THREE-story, brick-built Victorian villa was constructed in south London in the 1890s, and was recently redecorated and furnished for its owners by the influential London-based interior designer and antique dealer Christophe Gollut. Typical of many late Victorian English houses, it incorporates numerous Classical Revival fixtures and fittings. Prominent among these are several rather austere chimneypieces with simple, rectilinear jambs and friezes; a series of ornamental doorheads, each comprising a broken pediment and small entablature; and a diverse range of cornice moldings, the more elaborate of which feature egg-and-dart or stylized floral motifs. In addition, most of the rooms have picture and dado rails, which establish the tripartite division of the walls into frieze, field, and dado based on the Classical orders. As in numerous other Victorian houses, however, the architectural conceits are not all derived from the Classical

vocabulary of ornament. For example, the wooden casement windows with rectangular leaded lights recall 16th- and early 17th-century "Jacobethan" prototypes.

Christophe Gollut has sympathetically integrated these original fixtures and fittings within a new decorative scheme that exploits the great amount of natural light entering the house via its large windows. It recalls the lighter, brighter look that became increasingly fashionable (on both sides of the Atlantic) toward the end of the Victorian period. The effect is primarily achieved by leaving many of the windows undraped, and by employing a palette of pale greens, lighter stone colors, and shades of yellow and white as a backdrop for richer, darker Victorian shades of red and blue. These are largely confined to solid, densely patterned period upholstery fabrics, and are complemented throughout by the rich, lustrous yellow- and reddish-brown tones of mahogany furniture.

ABOVE The downstairs hall is given a much lighter decorative treatment than many of its mid-Victorian predecessors: the doors and wainscoting are painted a grayish-cream stone color, while the flat-plastered walls above are white. Classical references are evident in the entablature and broken pediment above the door.

FAR LEFT Illuminated by undraped casement windows, the built-in window seat in a living room features a vibrant red seat-cover and several colorfully patterned scatter cushions.

LEFT Off-white and cream colors provide a neutral backdrop for the vibrant blue jambs and lintel of the fireplace, and a finely figured polychrome marble tabletop.

ABOVE A two-tone pale green striped French wallpaper covers the library walls. The 19th-century sofa has a spectacular flame-cut mahogany back and is upholstered with a paisley fabric. These patterns include stylized pine cones and other plant-form motifs and were inspired by the imported Kashmiri shawls that were fashionable in Britain, France, and the United States during the late 19th century.

RIGHT This corner of the library displays a finely balanced interplay between lighter colors – including the white-painted ceiling and the off-white ground of the floral-patterned rug – and darker ones, including the red ground of the table-throw and the *faux* rosewood bookcases and fireplace.

*"It's a popular
misconception
that all Victorian
interiors were
dark and
gloomy."*

(Christophe Gollut, interior designer)

Above Classical references in the
main drawing room include a male
bust of white statuary marble
displayed on a *faux* porphyry
pedestal column.

Left The strong sense of space in
the well lit main drawing room is
enhanced by the white-painted
ceiling and architectural moldings
and by the use of light tones of green
in the papered and painted walls and
window drapes. These are balanced
by the richer and warmer hues –
mostly red and pink – that recur in
the eclectic mix of plain and
patterned upholstery and other
soft furnishings.

Using the Victorian palette

Although the Victorian era spanned well over half a century and accommodated numerous often eclectic styles of architecture and decoration (see pp.116–27), broad trends are discernible in the use of color. Prior to the 1850s, lighter Neoclassical hues, especially pale pink, almond, lilac, lavender, and iridescent white, remained fashionable, although darker colors such as crimson-red were used in "masculine" libraries and dining rooms. These were superseded in the third quarter of the 19th century by a stronger palette dominated by traditional, earthy reds and browns, vivid aniline greens, blues, purples, and yellows – and an extensive use of gilding. The last quarter of the century witnessed a reaction to this powerful polychromatic "High Victorian" palette, and the new decorative style developed lighter, more muted color schemes in which considerable use was made of milky yellows, ivory, olive-greens, rose-reds, pale blues, soft grays, and white.

RIGHT Late Victorian colors – white, gray-green, and stone – complement mahogany furniture and dusty pink, yellow, and crimson fabrics.

BELOW Contrasting colors were used on clapboarded Victorian houses: here the window frames of white-painted 1890s American rowhouses are picked out in bottle green.

ABOVE The wallpaper in the Goodwin Reception Room, at the Wadsworth Atheneum, Hartford, Connecticut, has a naturalistic floral pattern depicted in the muted, harmonious colors characteristic of many late 19th-century interiors.

LEFT The muted tertiary hues fashionable during the late Victorian era were often enlivened with more vibrant color, such as the blues in the top cover of this upholstered chair.

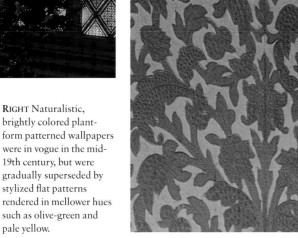

ABOVE Stained glass became very fashionable during the Victorian era. The perfection of plate-glass making techniques meant that larger panes could be made but, with the Gothic Revival, small leaded lights in casement windows were popular.

RIGHT Naturalistic, brightly colored plant-form patterned wallpapers were in vogue in the mid-19th century, but were gradually superseded by stylized flat patterns rendered in mellower hues such as olive-green and pale yellow.

RIGHT Wood-paneled rooms, popular in the Colonial period (see pp.36–53), enjoyed a revival in the late 19th century. This example, in the Wadsworth Atheneum, Hartford, incorporates a shell-domed cabinet.

BELOW LEFT & RIGHT Gilding was used on Victorian picture frames and to highlight moldings such as dado and picture rails. It also enriches and injects warmth into the color schemes.

FARROW & BALL
Light Gray · U/C10

FIRED EARTH/
PAINT PORTFOLIO
Aconite Yellow

FIRED EARTH/
PAINT PORTFOLIO
Morris Green

DULUX HERITAGE COLOURS
VICTORIAN (1837–1901)
Victorian 27

DULUX HERITAGE COLOURS
VICTORIAN (1837–1901)
Victorian 29

ACE ILLUMINATIONS
Timothy's Eyes 65–A

DULUX HERITAGE
Crimson

PAINT MAGIC/
JOCASTA INNES
Chinese Red

DULUX HERITAGE COLOURS
VICTORIAN (1837–1901)
Victorian 3

Modern style

RIGHT The Richard Mandel House in Westchester County, New York, by American architect Edward Durell Stone (1902–78), is typical of 1930s Modernism. Its emphasis on clean lines and horizontal planes is established by the use of flat roofs and decks, together with long bands of steel-frame casement windows and glazed doors set flush in walls of white-painted concrete.

RIGHT The Villa Savoye at Poissy, France, designed in 1928–9 by Charles-Edouard Le Corbusier (1887–1966), is a classic example of residential International Modern architecture. The plain, cubic shapes and horizontal planes of the interior – in white and neutral hues – are relieved by the curved surface of the spiral staircase, which also contributes to the asymmetry of the design.

ABOVE The horizontal aesthetic that dominates the Richard Mandel House's exterior is also clearly evident in its interior. On this staircase and landing, a neutral color scheme is combined with pale brown cork-tile floor covering. The polished aluminum balustrade, designed by Donald Deskey, contributes to the look known in the USA as "Stream-lined Moderne."

THE TERMS INTERNATIONAL MODERN and International Style were coined in the early 1930s. They were used to describe a new style of architecture that had been initiated before World War I by architects such as Adolf Loos, Frank Lloyd Wright, Josef Hoffmann, and Walter Gropius, and which subsequently developed between the wars (initially in Europe and then in the USA), notably through the work of Le Corbusier, Mies van der Rohe, and the Bauhaus school. In addition to promoting the virtues of industrial design (in which form served function) and of quality-controlled mass-production, the underlying rationale of most of the variants of Modernism was the desire to render the home, in the words of Le Corbusier, an efficient "machine for living in." In practice, this resulted in a pared-down architecture of steel, white-painted concrete, and large expanses of glass, in asymmetrical, unornamented cubic compositions. The emphasis was usually on horizontal rather than vertical planes, and much use was made of flexible, open-plan spaces, especially at ground level. The resulting streamlined look was often likened to the great ocean-going liners of the interwar years.

The shunning of "unnecessary" exterior and interior ornament, such as moldings, friezes, and dados, and the extensive use made of "new" materials, such as glass bricks, chromed steel, linoleum, and cork, were complemented by a decorative palette that made minimal use of color and pattern. This served not only to emphasize the form and texture of architectural fixtures and furnishings, but also to enhance a general sense of light and space (helped by the Modernists' generous use of glazing). For example, many rooms were painted all-white, or in off-whites such as ivory, cream, champagne, and dove-gray. Apart from neutral blacks, and occasional and small splashes of primary colors, other popular pale hues included buff, beige, coffee, and pastel blues, pinks, and greens.

ABOVE Modernist interiors are invariably light and spacious – a result of the use of large expanses of glazing and white and pale hues, and the absence of decorative moldings. The effect is enhanced in the open-plan living area of the Richard Mandel House by the clean lines of the "industrial design" furniture, made from glass, aluminum, and chromed steel.

THE RICHARD MANDEL HOUSE

NAMED AFTER ITS first owner, the Richard Mandel House is a fine example of residential American Modernist architecture in its purest form. Located on a 17-acre (6.8-hectare) site in Bedford Hills, Westchester County, New York, it was designed in 1931 by Edward Durell Stone and completed in 1934. The current owners, Nannette and Eric Brill, who describe themselves as temporary "caretakers," bought the property largely unaltered in 1991. They subsequently refurbished it to near-original condition, and the house became a National Landmark in 1996.

Set on three floors, occupying 10,000 square feet (900 square meters) and constructed from concrete, steel, and glass, the building reflects the strong horizontal aesthetic favored by many Modernist architects. The flat planes of the roofs, large decks and balconies, expanses of white-painted concrete, and glass set in steel-frame casement windows and doors emphasize the streamlined look. The only counterpoint to these unornamented, rectilinear forms occurs in the dining room, whose curved walls are made of semi-opaque glass bricks. These augment the high levels of natural light that enter via the large, drapeless, plate-glass windows and doors. In combination with the scale of the rooms (and an open-plan living area), this makes for an exceptionally bright and spacious interior.

The sense of light and space in all the rooms is substantially enhanced by their characteristically Modern decoration. Like the concrete outside, most of the plaster walls and ceilings are painted white, as are the flush-panel wooden doors. The four working fireplaces are either white or a pale beige stone color that contrasts with the black *terrazzo* hearths; in keeping with the original plans for the house, the Brills have covered the fireplace walls with

Above The dining room table was designed for the house by Donald Deskey in the early 1930s. Its white Bakelite top incorporates an illuminated glass panel. The green leather-upholstered dining chairs were designed in 1934 by Gilbert Rohde, another pioneer of industrial design in the U.S.

Below The all-white color scheme of the master bedroom comprises white-painted walls and ceiling, and the original white linoleum sheet flooring. The yellow lacquered *chinoiserie* bed, flanked by a pair of matching nightstands, is part of a bedroom set that also includes (unseen) a bench and a chest with green lacquered drawers. The set is not original to the house but was designed by Donald Deskey in the 1930s.

mirrors, which doubles the apparent size of the rooms. Apart from the highly distinctive black *terrazzo* floor in the dining room, the floor coverings are all pale, neutral hues: cork tiles in the living room, library, and hall; white linoleum in the master bedroom; ceramic or rubber tiles in the bathrooms, and plain carpet in guest quarters. The artificial lighting is equally unobtrusive; it comes from the flush panels in the ceilings and some shelving and tabletops, and from Modernist and Art Deco lamp-stands and wall fixtures.

Most of the lights – like the aluminum balustrade on the staircase and much of the furniture – were designed specifically for the house in the early 1930s by Donald Deskey, a pioneer of industrial design in the United States. Produced in materials such as chromed steel, aluminum, glass, natural and lacquered woods, and white or neutral-colored fabrics, their geometric forms and clean lines perfectly complement the dramatic Modernist architecture and decoration of the house.

Above Large expanses of mirror glass on the fireplace wall serve to increase the natural light in this open-plan living area, while also enhancing the sense of space. The plain-fronted beige stone fire-surround has a contrasting black *terrazzo* hearth and slips, and is typically Modernist in its slablike construction and lack of ornamentation. The pair of aluminum andirons in the hearth was designed by Donald Deskey, as was the grand piano reflected in the mirrors. The aluminum-framed white fabric-upholstered chair, and the chrome and glass table, are also by Deskey, designed *c*.1929 and produced by the Ypsilanti Reed Furniture Company.

ABOVE Illuminated in the day by steel-framed, plate-glass casement windows, and at night by circular lighting panels set flush into the ceiling, the tall, white-painted cement planter in the entrance hall contains various species of cacti (as it did when the house was first furnished). Their pale green, fawn, and buff colors are popular Modernist hues.

LEFT The original cork tile floor survives in the upstairs living room (and also in the library and halls). Cork tiles were often employed in Modernist houses. Favored alternatives included polished hardwoods (sometimes augmented by a rug of bold, abstract design); stone blocks; mosaics; *terrazzo*; linoleum; inlaid rubber, or plain wall-to-wall carpets.

Post-Modern style

RIGHT With its open-plan living area, white-painted concrete block walls, and industrial profile steel ceilings, the Flower House clearly shows the influence of "Industrial Modernist" architects. As elsewhere in this 1990s London townhouse, however, the neutral background palette of white and natural wood tones is enriched with Post-Modern splashes of color, seen here in the abstract painting by architect Peter Romanuik.

RIGHT Post-Modern decoration is characterized by a highly considered use of color. In the stair hall of Alexander and Meagan Julian's Arts and Crafts-style house in Ridgefield, Connecticut, large planes of coral pink and cornflower blue paint are juxtaposed to clearly define the configuration of the walls. Being of almost equal chromatic intensity, neither color "advances" or "retreats" at the expense of the other.

ABOVE The Ministry of Taste in Marrakesh is quintessentially Post-Modern in the way it artfully blends African desert colors and textures with diverse architectural and decorative motifs. These include Dogon "stickwork" and European-style columns and balustrades embellished with iron loops.

THE MODERN MOVEMENT, which flourished on both sides of the Atlantic, especially in the United States, between World Wars I and II, was well-intentioned in its ambition to give society a new, honest architecture for the 20th century. In theory, this meant breaking all stylistic links with the past, the clearest expression of which was the rejection of "superfluous" ornamentation. In practice, it resulted in an International Modern style characterized by predominently rectilinear, flat-roofed buildings with unadorned concrete and/or glass walls and metal-framed strip windows, decorated with a neutral palette of white and off-whites (see pp. 130–35).

Murmurings of discontent with the Modern style could be heard as early as the late 1940s. However, its perceived weaknesses were not rigorously exposed until the 1960s, most notably in two influential American publications. The first of these was Jane Jacobs's *The Death and Life of Great American Cities* (1961), which argued that many cities had been rendered architecturally incoherent by the inappropriate application of Modernist theories. The second was Robert Venturi's *Complexity and Contradiction in Architecture* (1966), with a central message that was loud and clear: refuting a central tenet of Modernism, Venturi declared that "less is a bore." More specifically, he argued that any building or interior reduced to puritanical geometric shapes lacked the valuable referential quality of historical architecture; it was, in effect, a sterile style of intellectual snobbery.

If Post-Modernism had a starting point, it was Venturi's book. Never a specific style, Post-Modernism was more an attitude and, more importantly, a general invitation for architects, designers, and decorators to embrace the past in an allusive way. After Venturi, color, decoration, and historical motifs were revalidated, as long as they were used in a spirit of conscious reference rather than of mindless replication.

ABOVE The Post-Modern rediscovery of the joys of color has been particularly evident in the treatment of upholstery fabrics. When Alexander Julian designed this set of leather-upholstered dining chairs for his house in Connecticut, he saw no need to restrict their color to the natural tones of the calfskin.

ABOVE When designing his home in Mexico City, architect Javier Sordo Madaleno reinterpreted ancient Mesoamerican forms using traditional and modern materials. The steps leading up to the entrance are cut from volcanic rock, flanked by pillars wound from thick steel cables.

ABOVE The eclectic choice of materials – canvas, concrete, glass, rubber, and enameled and chromed steel – in the bathing area of the Flower House is very Post-Modern.

ABOVE A revival of figurative ornament has been a notable feature of Post-Modern architecture and decoration. It often takes the form of sculptural artifacts, such as the metalwork bull that welcomes visitors to the inner courtyard of Javier Sordo Madaleno's house in Mexico City.

RIGHT The interaction between light and space is as relevant to Post-Modern architects as it was to their Modernist predecessors – but with the added dimension of color. The red door at the top of this staircase in Madaleno's home appears both to focus the light and to symbolize its source.

An early convert to Post-Modernism was the American architect Michael Graves, who began his career in the 1960s creating private houses in the austere Modernist tradition. In the early 1980s, however, he designed a Post-Modern icon: the Public Service Building in Portland, Oregon. This boldly stylized reworking of classical architectural elements such as colonnades and loggias was artfully suggestive of a child's colorful play-brick construction. The Portland building even has a friendly public "face," composed of stylized pilasters and keystones placed on the facade.

Another persuasive book from Venturi and a series of influential Post-Modern commentaries from the architectural critic Charles Jencks were to legitimize further this new enthusiasm for decorative allusion. Unrestricted by dogma or stylistic restrictions, Post-Modernism has spread its influence far and wide across the globe. For example, Mexico's flirtation with the International Style (which began in the 1920s) was superseded in the late 1960s by the rediscovery of Mesoamerican color and

LEFT Natural wood tones play a prominent role in Alexander and Meagan Julian's Arts and Crafts-style house. Cherry and maple have been used for most of the built-in and free-standing kitchen furniture. The lighter tones of the maple are then picked up on the walls, which are painted saffron yellow – an appropriately culinary color.

BELOW The polychrome *en-suite* color scheme in the Julians' dining room works particularly well because all the colors used – whether in the upholstery, decorative artifacts, or architectural fixtures and fittings – are of similar tonal value and chromatic intensity.

decoration – a development that echoed the cultural concerns of Post-Modernism elsewhere. In the United States, a renewed interest in the Arts and Crafts Movement of the late 19th and early 20th centuries reflected the acceptability of revisiting and reinterpreting past styles that were once thought redundant. In Morocco, central African motifs and colors have been sympathetically and wittily integrated into the legacy of colonial and indigenous North African styles of architecture. In Britain, Modernist townhouses, and in France 17th-century Baroque chateaux and 19th-century Parisian apartments have been inventively recolored and refurnished in the spirit of Post-Modern eclecticism. In short, Post-Modernism has given back what the Modernists took away. In the process, it has introduced an element of knowing artfulness that has spread beyond architecture and interior design to become a core component of the *Zeitgeist* of the late 20th and early 21st centuries.

LEFT Symbolic and decorative ornament have re-emerged in Post-Modern decoration along with color. In a bedroom in Madaleno's Mexico City home, beige walls and white pillows provide a neutral background for a vibrant yellow headboard and three floral-patterned pillows. They provide a luxurious contrast to the crucifix above.

THE MINISTRY OF TASTE

AN ESSENTIAL ELEMENT of Post-Modernism is the freedom to play sophisticated games with the forms, colors, and icons of past eras or other cultures. A home/studio/gallery in Marrakesh offers a fine example of how to reinvent traditional elements in the context of a modern domestic and commercial space. "The Ministry of Taste" is the creation of Alessandra Lippini and Fabrizio Bizzarri, who eschewed the local fashion for building homes based on historical notions of opulence and luxury, in favor of reinterpreting the rural colors and motifs of central Africa.

Since the three-story house also serves as an exhibition space and a studio for Lippini and Bizzarri's furnishing design service, art and artfulness are everywhere. The rooms are organized around a central courtyard where the traditional Moroccan fountain is replaced with another cooling water feature: a bathing pool. On the same level are a dining room, living room, eat-in kitchen, and bathroom. The second floor has two more living rooms and a bedroom, while on the top floor there is a large roof terrace crowned by an observatory tower.

It is the color and ornament, as much as the layout, however, that establish the building's links with an African heritage. From the ocher-hued observatory tower down to the umber-colored ground floor, everything is drawn from the palette of the desert – luminous yellows and browns, usually finished with rough, sandy textures. Walls and columns are decorated with native African symbols. Floors are of cement and mortar. Asymmetrical ceilings feature honeycomb recesses tinted with natural pigments. Fireplaces are constructed using river clay dressed with lime and oil. All this might suggest the straightforward recreation of traditional elements, if it were not for the designers' Post-Modern sensibilities that recast everything in a way that is at once surprising, allusive, and witty.

ABOVE Many wall-mounted ornaments on display at "The Ministry of Taste" were commissioned by Lippini and Bizzarri from local craftsmen. In a neutral Western interior they might be unduly prominent, but here, against the colors of the desert, they appear to blend harmoniously within the overall decorative scheme.

RIGHT Fireplaces provide the sole source of heat during the colder months of the year. This raised hearth is topped with antlerlike flues and flanked by a network of niches for storage and display; all are made from river clay dressed with oil and lime. The boldly organic lines of the fireplace and chimney lend it a totemlike look. The equally organic form of the shelving is repeated in the ceiling, where a honeycomb of hollows is decorated with a variety of natural pigments.

LEFT African symbols are used in relief to break up a solid expanse of yellow. A constant interplay between color and texture lies at the heart of the house, with the dynamics of that relationship substantially controlled by sunlight. The varying intensity of the light affects the luminosity of the color, and its varying angles at different times of the day determine the depth of the relief and texture.

RIGHT The courtyard galleries are supported on columns that feature iron rings around their bases – another reference to the tight-fitting necklaces worn by tribeswomen of the Sudan. The columns support wooden beams that look as if they might be encrusted with bright yellow lichen – a far cry from the smooth, calculated, antiseptic finish of the conventional Western rolled-steel joist.

A MESOAMERICAN REVIVAL

THE MEXICO CITY home of the influential Mexican architect Javier Sordo Madaleno was originally designed by his father, Juan Sordo, who sold it in 1979. Ten years later, Javier bought it back and totally remodeled the house, completing the project in 1992. The result is a particularly evocative example of Post-Modern Mexican architecture and decoration, demonstrating its renewed appreciation and reworking of pre-Hispanic Mesoamerican traditions, tailored to contemporary needs and aesthetics.

There is a tremendous sense of space, light, and color throughout the house. Decorated with a palette of mottled yellow-ochers and more vibrant yellows and orange-reds, offset against white and the natural colors of stone, marble, and wood, the generously proportioned, brightly illuminated courtyards, rooms, and corridors instantly recall Toltec and Aztec prototypes. This celebration of Mexico's precolonial cultural heritage is reinforced by numerous architectural motifs associated with Toltec and Aztec

BELOW A large alcove is partitioned off from the dining room (see opposite) by iron latticework screens. These were inspired by the rudimentary doors of interlaced bamboo often found in the simple vernacular architecture of rural Mexico. The stone pestle-and-mortar and the bundle of dried wheat sheaves symbolize the fruits of the Mexican harvest.

ABOVE The fountain courtyard is designated as a meditative space within the house. Open to the sky, it is bordered on three sides by high rendered walls, and on the fourth side by a massive steel-framed window that can be pivoted open and shut. The walls are painted yellow-ocher, which reflects warm light around the courtyard and out into the house. The calming properties of the fountain's cooling waters are enhanced by the river pebbles placed on the courtyard floor – the sound of water as it falls over and flows through them is reminiscent of a waterfall.

RIGHT Framed by bright yellow-painted walls, pre-Hispanic male and female idols peer out from the darker recess of a raised alcove at the foot of a staircase. They serve as potent symbols of the renaissance of interest in ancient Mesoamerican cultures, and of the substantial influence they have had on Post-Modern Mexican architecture, ornament, and decoration.

BELOW Light enters this upstairs corridor via a narrow inset window, which extends from the landing floor to the top of the side walls and continues as a skylight running along the middle of the curved ceiling. Bounced off rough-plastered walls that are ragged an ocher-orange hue, the light imparts a warm glow over the corridor's pegged-plank floor and central staircase wall. The latter is clad with marble and inset with uplighters that provide discreet illumination. In this rigorously geometric composition, the bold color contrast between the orange-red doors and the other surfaces is offset by the more subtle gradations of color created by changes in the intensity and direction of light at different times of day and night.

temples and palaces. These include slit windows and skylights to control the entrance of the powerful Mexican sunlight; an azure-blue courtyard lap pool; and long flights of stone steps rising and falling to different levels.

In typical Post-Modern style, Mexico's more recent colonial and, in turn, industrial history are also seamlessly accommodated: iron trellis screens evoke the bamboo doors of vernacular rural dwellings and celebrate Mexico's metalworking traditions; baroque chandeliers hang over the dining table; Pueblo tin-glazed earthenware adorns alcoves and tables; and, in the most ingenious fusion of past and present, the massive columns flanking the entrance to the house are wound with rugged industrial steel cables.

ABOVE Contrasted against a white ceiling and baseboards, the flat-plastered walls of the well-lit dining room are ragged a distinctive mottled orange-red color, which is echoed in the upholstery of the dining chairs. Made of robust pine, the chairs and dining table were designed by Javier Sordo Madaleno. The three baroque candelabra hanging above the table are a reminder of Mexico's Spanish colonial heritage.

FAUVIST FANTASY

THE PRIMARY SOURCE of inspiration for Alexander and Meagan Julian's cedar-shingled, five-story home in Ridgefield, Connecticut, was the Craftsman-style houses designed by the Pasadena architects Charles and Henry Greene during the early 20th century. Meagan Julian had first admired these while growing up in San Francisco's Bay Area. California architect John Marsh Davis has captured the essential characteristics of the Craftsman style, using beautiful woods and high-quality carpentry, and creating a strong sense of space, light, and continuity throughout the Julians' house. There are, however, two

ABOVE In the well-lit dining room, the crimson-red of the ceiling, dark indigo-blue of the picture frame, and rich brown tones of the woodwork are dynamically but seamlessly contrasted with the lighter, grayish-blue lavender colors of the floor covering, painted cabinet, paintings, and flowers.

LEFT & RIGHT The stairwell and upstairs gallery are a veritable "Fauvist fantasy" in which each architectural plane – whether painted or natural wood – is delineated with a different color of equal chromatic intensity to its neighbor. The paint colors are cornflower blue, coral pink, and chartreuse green.

notable Post-Modern developments of this particular Arts and Crafts model. The first is architectural: unlike Greene & Greene's low one- and two-story dwellings, this house is worked to a vertical aesthetic. This is demonstrated in a layout that runs up through five floors, and in the ceiling heights – up to 22 feet (6.7 meters) in the dining room.

The second, most distinctive development is the highly sophisticated use of color. With color consultants Donald Kaufman and Taffy Dahl, who custom-mix their own paints, the Julians drew on a decorative palette of 56 different hues to define not only individual rooms, but also their specific architectural configurations. The effect recalls the early 20th-century Fauvist paintings of Henri Matisse, in which spaces are boldly defined by formally ordered blocks of brilliant color. Moreover, by always juxtaposing paint colors and wooden fixtures, fittings, and furniture of equal chromatic intensity and luminosity, the Julians have created a thoroughly harmonious relationship between the decoration and the architecture. This holistic approach is in keeping with the Craftsman principles that inspired the design of the house in the first place.

ABOVE Paler pastel tones of green, yellow, and pink (the latter not shown here) are employed in the bedrooms. As in the receiving rooms of the house, the saturation and luminosity of these colors has been carefully chosen to match that of the wooden furniture and architectural fixtures.

ABOVE The ceramic surround of this raised bedroom hearth was designed by Constance Lesley of Rhode Island. Its distinctive check-pattern ground is embellished with naturalistic fruit and floral motifs.

THE FLOWER HOUSE

DESIGNED AND DECORATED by its owners, architect Peter Romanuik and florist Paula Pryke, the Flower House is surrounded by commercial and light-industrial buildings in north London, and was built on the site of an old garage-workshop. The influence of "Industrial Modernist" architects such as Richard Neutra and Pierre Koenig is clearly evident in its construction and layout: it has a steel frame, infilled with concrete blocks on three sides and glass on the front elevation; an open-plan living–dining area (with sequestered kitchen) that leads onto a California-style terrace; and, in keeping with the utilitarian style of the building and the history of the site, incorporates a flower workroom and internal garage on the ground floor.

The architectural fixtures and fittings – such as large horizontal panels of glass, rectilinear-pattern woodblock flooring, unbalustraded staircases, flat-paneled sliding doors, and white-painted corrugated steel ceilings and breeze-block walls – display an absence of ornament that is in keeping with the Modernist tradition. To soften and enrich the shell, however, Post-Modern splashes of bright, solid color were introduced throughout the house.

In the bedrooms and bathrooms, color has been applied to some of the architectural fixtures – notably the yellow, aquamarine, and royal blue of the sliding doors, which create elongated, solid planes of color when the doors are closed. In the living–dining area below, however, color is mainly restricted to the furniture, artifacts, and textiles. Prominent among these are a pair of red sofas, scattered with blue and yellow pillows; a pale blue dining table surrounded by lime-green, pale blue, mauve, yellow, and red chairs; a blue and white rug; and a large abstract painting beside the front door. An enormous green cactus next to the sofa provides a link with the profusion of flowers and foliage on the terrace outside.

ABOVE The architectural shell of the living area comprises an industrial profile steel ceiling and concrete block walls (both white-painted), sliding glass doors, and iroko strip flooring. This neutral-colored background is enlivened by color introduced by some of the furnishings and artifacts. The most prominent of these are the sofa and the large abstract painting. The sculptural qualities of the former are enhanced by a scarlet-red cotton-twill cover, and relieved by silk scatter cushions in royal blue and yellow. These primary colors are picked up in Peter Romanuik's painting, *Paula Picking Flowers*.

ABOVE Injections of color are provided in the master bedroom by the furnishings: a royal-blue cotton-upholstered bed, with large foot bolster, by Hitch Mylius; a multicolored check-pattern quilt from Heal's; silk-covered scatter cushions from Conran; and a sage green knotted-pile carpet. The physical link with the terrace, established by large sliding glass doors, is visually reinforced by the presence of green, yellow, and brown hues in these fabrics – colors inherent in the potted foliage outside. As in the living area downstairs, decorative coherence is also evident in the dominant colors of the paintings, by C. Lumato, which hang above the bed.

"…we introduced splashes of bright, solid color to enrich the house…to soften the effect and make it friendlier."

(Peter Romanuik and Paula Pryke)

ABOVE Iroko strip flooring extends from the living to the dining area, where the table and chairs stand on chromed steel legs. The gray-blue tabletop is a solid core laminate. The red, blue, and lime-green molded plywood chairs, known as "5701s," were designed in the 1950s by the Modernist Danish architect Arne Jacobsen.

LEFT Primary colors – red, yellow, and blue – also illuminate the other end of the living area. The link with the sunlit foliage on the terrace is apparent not only in the golden yellow silk pillows on the sofa but also in the plant-form imagery seen in the border of the knotted-pile rug – a pattern called "Sunrise in Arizona," which depicts cacti set against the desert sky. The glass-topped coffee table was designed by Matthew Hilton.

A PARISIAN APARTMENT

FRENCH DESIGNER Amélie Dillemann's small apartment is on the sixth floor of a turn-of-the-19th-century building in Paris, and the striking decorative scheme of its drawing room is the realization of her desire "...to live in an interior of bright red...a uniformly painted box." Because red is such an emotionally stimulating color, considerable thought and experiment were devoted to finding an appropriate shade. For example, crimson was rejected as being "too boudoirlike" while violet-red was felt to be too tragic or "*Sunset Boulevard.*" The eventual choice was a much brighter and more energising orange-red tone, matched to the distinctive shade of red adopted as a brand color by the famous French couture house, Hermès.

This vibrant orange-red tone was applied to the walls, doors, and built-in cabinets, and sparingly carried over *en-suite* to some of the lightshades and decorative artifacts, such as the small storage boxes; its provenance is acknowledged in the presence of a number of chic Hermès carrier bags dotted around the room. The intrinsic warmth of the color is consolidated by staining the pine floorboards pale red mahogany, by the choice of a rich chocolate-brown-colored silk taffeta for the drapes and some slipcovers, and by the installation of an antique brown leather chesterfield sofa. Similarly, the red itself serves, via close proximity, to enrich the gilding of the mantelpiece, overmantel mirrors, and a pedestal side-table.

BELOW A distinctive Hermès orange-red paint covers the drawing-room walls of the Parisian apartment belonging to innovative French designer Amélie Dillemann; it is also applied *en-suite* to the built-in cabinets flanking the mantelpiece. In order to lighten the room and increase the sense of space, the ceiling has been painted matte off-white, which is echoed in the hearth surround and the 1920s portrait.

LEFT Many of the components in the gigantic wall clock that dominates this end of the drawing room were made from cardboard, as are the ebony-colored and gilded pedestal tables flanking the clock, and the candelabrum in the foreground.

ABOVE Chocolate-brown silk drapes frame a portrait of an 18th-century French gentleman hung in an ebony-colored molded cardboard frame. The same fabric is employed as a slipcover on the armchair that sits beneath the painting.

More dramatically, the color contrasts created by the juxtaposition of the red with ebony-colored picture frames and tables, and with the off-whites of the ceiling, hearth surround, and large portrait painting, establish a strong sense of theater. This is given something of a surreal twist when one realizes that some of the architectural fixtures and pieces of furniture, and many of the decorative artifacts, aren't quite what one expects them to be: the mantelpiece isn't stone, the mirror-frame moldings aren't *gesso*, the picture frames and side-tables aren't wood, and the mechanics of the wall clock aren't uniformly brass: all were in fact made by Amélie Dillemann from cardboard.

RIGHT The drawing-room mantelpiece, with its distinctive serpentine-profile frieze, is French neoclassical in style. Like the overmantel mirror frames, it is fashioned from cardboard and finished in antiqued gold leaf. The hearth is floored with variegated brown and white marble bordered by a plainer white-vein marble.

A FRENCH CHATEAU

LOCATED IN NORTHERN FRANCE, in a rural landscape of gently rolling hills, this palatial chateau was built in the early 17th century, its construction spanning the end of Henri IV's reign (1589–1610) and the early years of Louis XIII's (1610–1643). The exterior of the U-shaped building reflects – particularly in its decorative details – the rather austere, post-Renaissance French classicism of the period, which was to be superseded by the more flamboyant and ornate baroque style that flourished later in the 17th century under the patronage of Louis XIV.

In contrast, the interior of the chateau displays a number of different styles in its surviving architectural fixtures and fittings. For example, many of the *salons* were remodeled between 1720 and 1730, a period in which rococo ornament (see pp.54–9) was the height of fashion in France. Similarly, French neoclassical taste (see pp.64–9) is also represented in rooms refurbished in the late 18th century. However, the most recent changes were begun in the late 1980s by the architectural historian and interior designer Andrew Allfree, working with his companion and current owner of the chateau, David Moses.

It was a massive undertaking, much of the chateau having fallen into a state of near-ruin, but Allfree – a descendant of Alfred the Great, the ninth-century king of Wessex – has undoubtedly succeeded in restoring it to its former glories. This was, however, no simple restoration of the past, but rather a uniquely Post-Modern development in what he sees as the on-going evolution of the building.

LEFT Interior designer Andrew Allfree's sobriquet for this living room is the Departure Lounge – partly because of the bright red *banquette* seating, and partly because it is a room that people walk through on their way to somewhere else on the ground floor. Its walls are painted a saturated blue-green turquoise, a color originally introduced to the West from Persia, via Turkestan.

"Proportion and quality are more important than date." (Andrew Allfree)

LEFT The 18th-century paneling in the dining room is painted a vibrant absinthe-green. The giltwood overmantel mirror-glass and picture panel above the double-doors are Louis XV, as are the serpentine-profile marble chimneypiece and the crystal chandelier. The campaign dining table, laid with platinum-glazed pottery, is English Regency.

ABOVE The neoclassical wall paneling in this drawing room dates to the early 18th century. The wooden columns, which are painted a stone colour, were imported from a ruined neoclassical villa in New York state. The armchairs are voluptuously carved and upholstered in the baroque style. The chandelier is William IV.

BELOW The pinkish-red color used on the walls of this guest bedroom is known as cobalt violet, and is contrasted with the wood color applied to the doors, dado paneling, and overmantel mirror frame. The green hue of the pair of baluster-shaped vases on the early 19th-century French mahogany *secrétaire* provides a contrast to the pinkish-red on the walls.

RIGHT & BELOW RIGHT The walls above the dado paneling in the breakfast room are painted a vibrant, reflective, oil-based chrome yellow. In contrast, the paneling, window frames, and doors (unseen here) are painted a matte-finish bluish-gray color. The acanthus-leaf molding on the corner of the wall is an example of the Rococo-style ornament found in the house.

Allfree's approach to the project was fueled by a number of firmly held beliefs about the appropriate role of the restorer–interior designer working with old buildings. Above all, he is an advocate of, whenever possible, either salvaging original fixtures and fittings in their entirety, or seamlessly integrating what remains of them with the best-quality reproduction work. His rigorous approach – which, for earlier projects, earned him the honor of receiving the French order of Chevalier des Arts et des Lettres – is reflected throughout the restoration. For example, to insure accuracy of architectural detail, he insisted that early 17th-century lead decorations missing from the exterior were recast on site from those that had survived – a process that, together with the extensive repairs to the original slate roof, took several years. Similarly, he went to great lengths to preserve as much as possible of the wall-paneling, floorboards, window frames, and other woodwork, and employed highly skilled carpenters and paint finishers to blend new sections in with the old. Also, when reglazing the windows and interior mirrors, he sourced authentic period glass, with its distinctive green tint, rather than use inappropriate brighter, "whiter," and less expensive modern plate glass.

ABOVE LEFT A pale-brown oil-based paint was brushed directly onto the plaster wall (rather than on lining paper) above the dado paneling in Andrew Allfree's ground-floor office. The designer describes the color used on the paneling as "tractor green."

ABOVE RIGHT The walls above the dado paneling in Andrew Allfree's bedroom are painted with china-blue matte latex. The blue is echoed in the carpet and contrasted with the red velvet throw on the sofa. Pale natural wood tones also play a subtle role in the color scheme.

This meticulous, respectful approach to the restoration of extant architectural fixtures is accompanied, however, by a far more liberal attitude to redecoration and refurnishing. In these areas, Allfree does not believe in pursuing what Osbert Lancaster, the English cartoonist, stage designer, and writer (1908–86), described as "the fatal will-o'-the-wisp of period accuracy." In other words, trying to replicate original color schemes and furnishings is all too often doomed to failure and, moreover, is an unnecessarily unimaginative exercise in a home – as opposed to in a museum. Given the evolutionary nature of buildings and their decorations, it is just as valid, and much more exciting, to take into account the historical perspective, but to look at it through totally modern eyes. Put into practice, this belief has resulted in a spectacular series of dynamically colorful interiors that have collectively breathed new life into the old building.

RIGHT The wall paneling in the entrance hall incorporates a corner cupboard above a built-in seat; the interior of the cupboard is painted a Chinese lacquer red that provides the backdrop for a gilded earthenware dinner set. The black and white diamond-pattern stone tile floor is original to the house, although sections of it had to be replaced during the recent redecorations.

LEFT In this bedroom, lime-green-painted walls are contrasted with a white-painted ceiling and dado paneling. The sleeping alcove is defined by broad painted black and white vertical stripes. The combination of colors is rather reminiscent of a 1950s milliner's hatbox .

Allfree's decorative palette encompasses the rich reds, yellows, and blues used in the grander polychromatic color schemes of the 17th century; the brighter, more vivid hues, such as citron, violet, and turquoise, favored in the second half of the 18th century; and the sharp yellows, deep blues, acid greens, and crimson reds of the early-to-mid-19th century. Particularly notable are the turquoise walls and ceiling of a downstairs living room; the Veronese green wall paneling in the dining room; the chrome-yellow walls in the breakfast room; the cobalt-violet and china-blue walls in two of the other bedrooms; and the Chinese lacquer red of a display cupboard.

This is by no means the whole picture, however, as the 20th century also makes a significant contribution to the palette. For example, a dark "tractor-green" has been applied to the dado paneling in a ground-floor office; built-in cupboards in the kitchen are painted blackish-blue mixed to the color of a British policeman's uniform; and in another bedroom the black and white striped alcove, flanked by lime-green walls, conjures up images of milliners' hatboxes from the 1950s.

ABOVE The large half-tester bed in Andrew Allfree's bedroom (see also p.153, top right) is a type that originated in France in the 17th century. Characterized by a half- or, as here, full-length "flying" canopy suspended from a frame or the wall behind the headboard (rather than from corner posts), this type was also known in France as a *lit d'anges* or *lit à l'impériale*.

LEFT Concessions to modern living are rarely hidden at the chateau, but are usually carefully coordinated with the rest of the decor. Here in the dining room (see also p.151, bottom left), a telephone is prominently positioned on a leather-upholstered side-chair, the green of its plastic body and receiver closely matched to the Veronese green wall paneling.

ABOVE The finely figured *secrétaire* in the Departure Lounge (see also p.151) is 19th-century Biedermeier. Its semicolumnar plinth top is used to display a black and "gold" Etruscan-style vase. The *secrétaire* is flanked by a pair of gilt sconces on the wall, their shades fabricated by Andrew Allfree from brown paper bags. The two elaborately carved side-chairs with cabriole legs are Spanish and date to the mid-19th century.

RIGHT Boldly contrasted with the china-white of the bathroom fixtures and a white-framed vanity mirror, these bathroom walls are painted strong, vibrant cobalt blue. The slab of purple marble employed as splash protection above the sink resembles a fragment from classical antiquity.

Also, unlike many other restorers and interior decorators, Allfree does not feel bound by the dogma of period authenticity to use traditional formulations such as egg tempera on 17th-century interior woodwork, or old-fashioned distemper washes on pre-20th-century plaster walls. Indeed, he has a refreshingly pragmatic approach to the choice of pigments and paint mediums. Specifically, he prefers to exploit the purity and saturation of color offered by artists' oils which, cut with turpentine, also provide a very durable finish. However, he is not totally averse to using commercial oil-based house paints, or synthetic latex-emulsions. Nowadays, most of them provide excellent opacity and chromatic intensity, and are available in a tremendous range of tints and shades. As he says: "good color is where you can find it."

The Post-Modern panache of Allfree's decorating is also evident in his choice of furniture, artifacts, and fabrics. These are sourced from different countries and periods, and are deployed according to compatibility of scale, form, color, and ornamentation, rather than specific style or date. In a grand drawing room, for example, late 17th-century baroque armchairs, an early 18th-century rococo table, and a mid-18th-century *duchesse* are grouped under an early 19th-century William IV chandelier. In a living room, the characteristically austere German Biedermeier *secrétaire* is flanked by the voluptuous carvings on the backs and

> *"The most useful way to look at an old building is to understand that it is always evolving."* (Andrew Allfree)

cabriole legs of a pair of mid-19th-century Spanish side-chairs. In a small anteroom, a French pictorial tapestry dating to c.1700 hangs near a 19th-century Mexican-colonial pressed-tin mirror frame. The bed in the lime-green and black. and white striped "1950s hatbox-style" bedroom is dressed with a 19th-century red and white printed-cotton French bedspread. In the principal dining room, the 18th-century Veronese green wall paneling is contrasted with a sumptuous blue and gold damask *banquette*. These and other juxtapositions and combinations might be stylistically eclectic in terms of period, but they are always aesthetically harmonious, and just as significantly, they are representative of the evolution of styles and fashions that the chateau has accommodated through many earlier centuries.

ABOVE In this bathroom, the turquoise-green plaster walls and ceiling are combined with a matte dark blue door and dado paneling. The exterior of the enameled cast-iron, rolltop bathtub with lions'-paw feet is painted black, *en-suite* with the large wall mirror.

CHAPTER 3

National &
Regional
Palettes

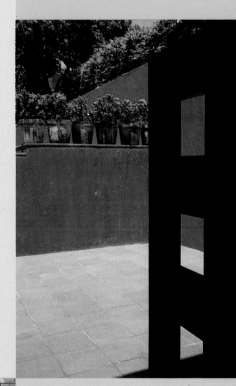

ABOVE A view across the adobe-walled courtyard of a house designed by architect Juan Carlos Braniff in the lakeside resort of Valle de Bravo, outside Mexico City.

LEFT An exterior fresco-plastered wall, stone-framed window and terracotta-tiled terrace at the Villa di Argiano, Montalcino, near Siena, Italy.

OPPOSITE Part of the colonnaded internal courtyard of Dâr Zellij, a recently restored 18th-century townhouse in the medina (old town) of Marrakesh, Morocco.

Tuscan style

RIGHT Sited next to a 16th-century church in the small village of Argiano, near Montalcino, this stone-built Tuscan house was constructed in 1798 for the local priest. It has been sympathetically renovated by the current owners, Guigi Maria Sesti and his wife Sarah, using stone, bricks, terracotta tiles, marble, and lumber from the surrounding area.

RIGHT The multivocational Guigi Maria Sesti is a winemaker and painter (refining and mixing his own pigments) who also likes to study the stars. His astronomical and artistic activities are reflected in the two-tone-blue color scheme in his writing room off the church at Argiano – it has a darker blue for the wooden ceiling boards and rafters, and a paler blue for the plastered walls.

ABOVE The primary sources of the Tuscan color palette are the distinctive burnt umber-, burnt sienna-, terracotta- and ocher-colored soils and clays of the region. These provide paint pigments and are also fired to make bricks and tiles. Other typical Tuscan colors are inspired by indigenous plants.

THE CENTRAL ITALIAN province of Tuscany has made an enormous contribution to the development of civic and ecclesiastical architecture, ornament, and decoration since the Middle Ages. In particular, its cities of Siena, Pisa, and, especially, Florence are the sites of some of Europe's most admired Gothic and Renaissance palaces and churches, many of which were conceived or remodeled between the 13th and 16th centuries by influential architects such as Arnolfo di Cambio, Pisano, Brunelleschi, Alberti, Michelangelo, and Vasari. The stature of Tuscany's grand Medieval and Renaissance urban buildings endures, and in the 21st century they remain a considerable source of architectural and decorative inspiration. However, these grand historical edifices are by no means all that Tuscany has to offer in that respect; and moreover, they do not constitute what has become known as "Tuscan style" – a description that relates to the rustic vernacular architecture of the region.

Tuscan style first gained international recognition during the 1950s, when Italian city dwellers began to redevelop traditional Tuscan farmhouses and outbuildings as country retreats – an ongoing phenomenon similar to the regeneration of country cottages, *manoirs*, and log-built lodges in, respectively, Britain, France, and the United States. The fundamental appeal of all such houses is their rural location, which in the case of Tuscany embraces a hilly landscape of ivory and yellow chalkstone, and umber- and ocher-colored soils and clays, covered with woodlands, grapevines, olive and lemon groves, and a profusion of wild and cultivated flowers and herbs.

The fabric and colors of the countryside, which has remained largely unchanged for centuries, are immediately evident in both the construction and the decoration of the buildings. Most of the houses are solidly built from local stone, with exterior walls stuccoed

ABOVE The pale blue walls in the upstairs hall of the Sestis' priest's house are designed to be both relaxing and invigorating. The fixtures and fittings are defined by contrasting colors: natural wood tones in the door and ceiling rafters, a darker blue wash for the baseboards, and burnt-sienna-colored floor tiles.

BELOW In Tuscan vernacular architecture, the practice of using constructional and decorative components (such as bricks, stucco render, and terracotta tiles, pots, and urns) made from local clays establishes an almost organic relationship between the buildings and the surrounding countryside. A profusion of flowers and foliage, as seen here, can often heighten the effect.

RIGHT Lavender grows in abundance throughout the Tuscan countryside, and is the inspiration for many of the pale lilac and grayish-blue hues often employed in Tuscan houses. Here, on the living room walls of Le Fontanelle farmhouse cottage near Montalcino, a lavender-blue distemper wash provides a color-coordinated backdrop for the display of decorative artifacts on the marble mantelpiece.

RIGHT Like many Tuscan interiors, the upstairs living room at Sarah and Guigi Maria Sesti's refurbished priest's house in Argiano emanates a feeling of both formality and comfort. The formal qualities of the high-ceilinged room are enhanced by a pale green colorwash on the walls that accentuates the sense of space. Comfort is provided by the cream-colored upholstered sofa, and in the rust-red and cream wool carpet.

in shades of soft ocher or dusky pink. Similarly, external walkways and terraces are made of stone slabs, rust-red bricks laid on end, or like the roof coverings, terracotta tiles baked from Tuscan clay. Inside, rooms are generously proportioned and usually have high ceilings. The sense of spaciousness is most evident in ground-level rooms with brick-vaulted ceilings (which originally would have been used to stable animals), and in converted shed buildings that once stored grain or olives.

Interior decoration also draws heavily on the palette of the landscape. Terracotta tiles, laid in simple geometric patterns, are the common flooring material, and are sometimes augmented with straw-colored woven mat, flat-weave rugs, or more rarely, knotted-pile carpets. Ceilings are either of flat plaster or exposed beams and rafters with infills of plaster or wooden ceiling boards; the plaster is usually painted white, although sometimes tints of blue or green are also used. Plastered walls are

"Tuscany looks the way Italy ought to look…"

(Johann Wolfgang von Goethe, poet, 1788)

LEFT The use of paint to simulate architectural details is a feature of some Tuscan houses: this *faux* dado rail is in a corridor at Le Fontanelle farmhouse cottage. The refinement of the painting is typically Tuscan: the muted yellow "rail" is precisely defined by thin gray-black bands, and the division of the wall further accentuated by the use of lighter and darker tones.

BELOW The mellow, earthy hues at the heart of the Tuscan palette are well represented in the entrance hall of Le Fontanelle farmhouse, where they can be seen in the brickwork of the vaulted ceiling, in the pale terracotta-tiled floor, and in the yellow-ocher distemper wash on the walls. The pale blue paint of the battened-plank door complements these earthy tones.

traditionally finished with distemper washes. Warm, earthy colors include yellow-ochers and pale rust-reds; grayish-blue lavender, and green-tinted whites are popular cooler hues. There is also a tradition in Tuscany of occasionally using paint (in subtle variations of the wall color) to simulate architectural features such as baseboards, dado rails, and moldings.

Tuscan-style furniture is eclectic, but in the spacious rooms its effect is rarely cluttered. Traditional rustic pieces include chairs, sofas, tables, and cupboards made from indigenous hardwoods, frequently chestnut, or from softwoods. The latter are either colorwashed or painted with motifs that simulate expensive marquetry inlay – a technique known as *arte povera*. Other items, notably beds, are constructed from wrought iron, while antler-frame tables and chairs are common. Many homeowners have also successfully introduced more sophisticated antique furniture, notably neoclassical pieces made from finely figured woods such as mahogany, walnut, or cherry.

Simple geometric patterns, such as stripes and chevrons, are favored for upholstery fabrics and bedcovers, especially in color combinations of yellow with reds or blues, and reds with greens. Plain fabrics in pinkish tones, creams, or off-whites are also popular, these colors being the usual choice for sheer cotton cloth hung up at windows and suspended over beds.

The use of cotton sheers or slatted wooden shutters – and sometimes both – to diffuse sunlight (which can often be intense in Tuscany during the summer months) and to cool an interior has a subtle impact on the decorative palette: individual colors tend to appear mellower, and the contrasts between them – notably between reds and greens, and between blues and yellows – are softened and made easier on the eye. This mellow feel reinforces the sense of comfort and relaxation that is inherent in even the largest, most formally furnished rooms – a quality that has helped promote Tuscan style not only in other parts of Italy but also in overseas markets.

LE FONTANELLE

RIGHT The walls in the dining room – like those in many of the other rooms at Le Fontanelle – are painted with a yellow ocher distemper colorwash by Adam Alvarez. The walls harmonize with the natural wood tones of the table and chairs, while the blue-gray portraits on the wall and the painted side-chairs complement the tableware in blue-tinted and clear glass.

BELOW A neoclassical bust, carved from white statuary marble, is displayed on the piano.

L E FONTANELLE farmhouse is located in the Tuscan countryside near the hilltop village of Montalcino, not far from Siena. Originally a rather dull, utilitarian dwelling, in which animals were stabled on the ground floor and the human occupants lived and slept on the floor above, it was purchased 16 years ago by Italian architect Piero Castellini Baldissera, who works out of Milan. Together with his son Nicolò, a London-based interior designer, he gradually transformed it and an adjacent cottage into a comfortable but stylish rural retreat from the hectic pace of city life.

The extensive gardens laid out at the beginning of the project have thrived due to the locality's plentiful water supply, which also gave rise to the name of the house: Le Fontanelle translates as "little fountains." Dotted with terraces, arbors, and gazebos, and filled with lush grass and a profusion of plants – notably grapevines and various species of climbing rose – they have a cultivated yet natural quality that is carried over into the architectural and decorative components of the house itself.

Natural materials – seen in unplastered, vaulted brick ceilings, distempered plaster walls, and terracotta floor tiles – are employed extensively throughout. They are derived from the same source as many of the pigments used in the decorator's palette: the idyllic Tuscan landscape familiar to us from numerous Italian Renaissance paintings.

The sienna, umber, copper, yellow-ocher and ocher-red soils and clays native to the region are immediately evident in the paints, washes, and upholstery fabrics – as are the luminous pale ivory and warm yellow hues of the local chalkstone, which is known as *alberese* and is used to construct the walls of nearby fortified hilltop towns. The greens and browns of surrounding oak and chestnut woodlands, alternating with rows of cypress trees, vines, and olive groves, also play a significant role – as does the Tuscan sky, in all its guises: near-white tinged with ocher, rust, and yellow when the land is shrouded in mist; pure, transparent blue under a midday summer sun; and a distinctive pale purple and lavender at dusk.

RIGHT The piano at Le Fontanelle is purely decorative – its strings and hammers have been gutted – and was bought for the highly distinctive figuring and mellow patina of its walnut-veneered case. On the wall behind is a neoclassical *bas-relief* of a Roman goddess, surrounded by an oval medallion; its terracotta-colored frame incorporates ribbons and strings of husks swagged-and-tailed from a pair of rosettes.

BELOW In this bedroom, which is reached via an outside staircase, the yellow-ocher distemper wash on the walls has been carried over onto the plaster ceiling panels between the exposed rafters. The rafters themselves, like their supporting beams, are painted in a yellow that is echoed in the striped curtains and bedcovers. The tiered corner stand (or "whatnot"), in mahogany, displays flowers picked from Le Fontanelle's gardens.

The primary consequence of using this spectrum of colors is the harmonious integration of the house with its environs – an effect that never looks contrived, and is reinforced by the furnishings. Particularly prominent are the late 18th-century Directoire chairs and settees made in Lucca; *arte povera* painted chairs and cabinets from Veneto and the Aldo Adige; moose-antler chairs (in homage to the hunting traditions of the region); and various 19th-century and modern pieces upholstered with traditional fabrics from Piero's textile business, C&C – also used for many of the window drapes and bedcovers.

The decorative artifacts are equally symbiotic. These include Italian glassware; specimen Italian marble; architectural tools and instruments owned by the famous 1930s Italian architect Piero Portaluppi; landscape and topographical prints; and neoclassical sculptures reflecting Tuscany's leading role in the revival of classical architecture, ornament, and decoration since the Renaissance.

ABOVE The main bedroom in Le Fontanelle's farmhouse cottage is dominated by a large four-poster bed with a military-style canopy and a pair of shield-back upholstered headboards. The two-tone striped bedcovers and hangings are made from a fabric that comes from owner Piero Castellini Baldissera's C&C line. The golden-yellow stripes complement the Tuscan ocher walls and paler lemon-yellow sheers at the windows, while the alternating grayish-blue stripes strike a cooler note.

ABOVE RIGHT Two-tone stripes are also used on the walls of one of the farmhouse bedrooms. The more muted colors of this hand-painted finish are picked up on the upholstered Lucca Directoire side-chair, and also in the hangings and covers (from the C&C collection) on the Rajasthani wrought-iron bed.

RIGHT A collection of specimen marble columns and balls is displayed in the main drawing room; most of the marble is indigenous to the region.

RIGHT Terracotta-colored walls provide the backdrop to an 18th-century Lucca Directoire daybed in another bedroom at Le Fontanelle farmhouse. The striped upholstery features alternating bands of yellow and pale and dark pink, while the pillow covers are golden yellow and burnt orange. The *faux marbre*-framed prints above the daybed show groups of figures at play in rural landscapes. Such idealized pastoral imagery was fashionable through much of Europe during the 18th century.

"As an artist, Piero is always looking for new projects, a fresh canvas on which to try out new ideas."

(Nicolò Baldissera)

ABOVE Diffused by sheer white cotton drapes, Tuscan sunshine gently illuminates the corridor between the living room and bedroom–bathroom in the farmhouse cottage at Le Fontanelle. Shades of yellow on the walls and woodwork also brighten the space, while off-white and pale and gray blues help keep down the heat.

LEFT Originally a stabling area, Le Fontanelle's drawing room retains its exposed vaulted ceiling of local brick. Punctuated by white-painted woodwork, its walls have a complementary yellow-ocher wash, enlivened by pinkish-reds in the upholstery.

Using the Tuscan palette

The core colors of the Tuscan palette are yellow-ocher, burnt sienna, umber, terracotta, and copper. On walls, these earthy, muted hues are traditionally applied in water-based matte-finish washes – which produce subtle gradations of color across their surfaces – rather than as solid blocks of color. They also recur in a more reflective, vibrant form in the polished natural wood tones (especially chestnut and walnut) of furniture, and in upholstery fabrics. Other warm colors, largely confined to fabrics, include reddish-pink and rust red. Apart from white, which is often used on ceilings, and the grayish-black of Tuscan wrought-iron furniture, the most popular cooler hues are the various shades of green and blue that can be found in native Tuscan plants. Prominent examples of these are thyme and olive green, and lilac and lavender blue.

RIGHT The harmonious relationship between decoration and furnishings that is characteristic of Tuscan style is primarily achieved through color coordination. Here, tones of warm yellow-ocher can be seen on the walls, the picture frame, the glazed jug, and the wooden table.

BELOW Using foliage to filter sunlight is a way of cooling exterior walkways. Shadows reduce the reflectivity of whitewashed surfaces.

ABOVE The painted patterns often seen in Tuscan houses mostly use simple, repeated geometric forms. Striped and zigzag chevron patterns, as in this bathroom, are especially popular; their original source was the military banners and bunting historically associated with this part of Italy.

LEFT Tuscan exteriors are dominated by earth colors derived from local soils and clays. Warm hues are displayed in brickwork, tiles, and stucco. The pale blue seen here on the doors, shutters, and window frames is inspired by the lavender that grows abundantly in these parts.

ABOVE Verdant native plants not only help to cool Tuscan interiors, but also provide an important visual and olfactory link with the surrounding countryside. These plants are displayed in locally-made pots on a traditional terracotta-tile floor.

RIGHT Although made from rustic materials, Tuscan vernacular houses are not lacking in elegance. Subtly contrasting hues are used to define features – here, a brick arch, doors, and fanlight – and to enhance the symmetry of their proportions.

FIRED EARTH/ PAINT PORTFOLIO Mineral Gray

DULUX COLOUR SELECTOR Natural Hessian

ROSE OF JERICHO Saffron

ACE ILLUMINATIONS Peanut Brittle · 84–D

CROWN EXPRESSIONS Clementine · CL–10

PAINT MAGIC/ JOCASTA INNES Etruscan Red

ABOVE Typical Tuscan colors such as yellow-ocher (seen here on the walls) and pinkish-reds (in the chair- and bedcovers) radiate a gentle warmth when illuminated by sunlight diffused through cotton sheers. The mix of furniture – wrought-iron table, bamboo side-chair, walnut-veneered headboard – is also typically Tuscan.

RIGHT The coherence of this Tuscan decorative scheme is underpinned by the color coordination of the wall finishes and the furnishings. Tones of the dominant hues – yellow and ocher – recur on the walls, the drapes, the pillows, the upholstery, and the bedcover.

ROSE OF JERICHO Tuscan Red

ROSE OF JERICHO Medici Blue

ROSE OF JERICHO Assisi Blue

Mexican style

RIGHT A pavilion and poolside area in the grounds of the restored 19th-century Hacienda de San Antonio, in Colima, Mexico. The small pavilion building has been painted in the ubiquitous *rosa Mexicana* (Mexican pink) to link it visually to the similarly colored exterior of the main house (see opposite). The earthy hues of the paving tiles on the terrace, like the reddish-brown natural wood tones of the patio furniture, also serve to tie the architecture, decoration, and furnishing of this area to the palette of the surrounding countryside.

ABOVE From the time of the Spanish conquest until independence in 1821, Mexico was part of the viceroyalty of New Spain. Understandably, European-style architectural forms – such as this niched figure on the corner of a building in Mexico City – abound, but they are often combined with a distinctly Mexican use of color.

THE VISUAL STYLE of Mexico is one in which form and color appear to be inseparable elements. Vibrant color is the emotional thread that runs throughout the long and varied architectural history of a country characterized by dramatic extremes of terrain, climate, and fortune. If it came as a shock to 19th-century historians to discover that the ancient Greek temples had been polychrome and not white as previously believed, it seems unimaginable that the buildings of Mexico could ever have been anything but suffused with color. From the vast volcanic stucco Pyramids of the Sun and the Moon in the ancient city of Teotihuacán (200B.C.–750A.D.) – each originally painted a single dominant hue, red and ocher respectively – to the work of 20th-century Mexican architects such as Luis Barragán, José de Yturbe, Manuel Mestre, and Juan and Javier Sordo Madaleno, color has been a visceral part of Mexico's built environment and remains intrinsic to the country's sense of self. The psychological impact of color, however, is rarely determined by the qualities of pigment alone. Scale of application is also crucial, and contemporary Mexican style often manages to look effortless in its interplay of color, space, and volume. This is due in part to the enduring influence of a dominant Mexican building form: the hacienda.

Haciendas were estates, originally bestowed upon favored *conquistadors*. They frequently outgrew their ranch-style origins to become huge self-contained feudal townships designed and developed as living monuments to the *hacendados* who ruled them. Many were destroyed in the Mexican uprising of 1910, but surviving examples continue to inspire contemporary designers with the harmony of their courtyards, with their massive wall placements and pillars, their richly detailed interiors and, of course, their resonant colors. But color, like architectural space, is nothing without light. Mexican

ABOVE In Mexico City, a pale-blue-painted facade with white, terracotta, and stone-colored detailing reflects a love of the decorative. The exuberant Spanish Baroque style, with its rich surface textures and detail, exerted a lasting influence in many of Spain's colonies, not least upon the haciendas and grand townhouses of Mexico.

LEFT The notion of a pastel-pink stately home is not at all incongruous in the Mexican architectural palette. Centerpiece of a 5,000-acre (2,000-hectare) plantation, the manor house of the Hacienda de San Antonio was renovated in 1978 by Mauricio Romano.

BELOW One of the Hacienda de San Antonio's guest rooms. The contemporary restoration has retained the rich pattern and texture of the traditional hacienda bedroom, while using a low, restful chromatic range.

style, in common with that of many other countries with hot climates, often seeks to blur the boundaries between inside and out, between artificial illumination and mediated daylight. In this way a secluded chapel mixes filtered daylight from high windows with its internal candlelight or an area for entertaining is located beneath the overhang of a patio roof, bounded by a row of stone columns opening out onto an open courtyard. Just as a distinctive red pigment is made from local clay and oil, Mexican man-made style invariably seems to reflect and blend with the surrounding landscape.

An enduring sense of style and color has allowed Mexico to celebrate its national spirit with remarkable consistency throughout a long and turbulent history. In doing so, it has given the rest of the world a unique perspective on the infinite possibilities of color.

LEFT In architecture and decoration, scale can often be as important as color. This modern bedroom interior at the Hacienda de San Antonio features an unusually long, wide bed specifically made to suit the proportions of the room. The bed linen was custom-made in Mexico City, its pinkish-red hue married to that of the floor covering. Equally harmonious is the use of a yellow and ocher mottled wash on the walls – colors derived from the exposed brickwork of the vaulted ceiling.

"Mexico…it's the only place where, when I get there, I don't want to be anywhere else." (Robert Couturier, architect)

LEFT The dishes in the dining room of the Hacienda de San Antonio were commissioned from Puebla potters, and feature a pineapple motif that is picked up in the pattern of the Portuguese carpet. The dining room embodies a sense of occasion that owes much to its well-proportioned barrel-vaulted brick ceiling. The Hacienda's most recent renovator, French architect Robert Couturier, used artisans from Guanajuato to construct the ceiling as part of a general expansion and renovation program in the late 1980s. "It was remarkable to watch them construct that ceiling," remarks Couturier. "They weren't engineers…they did it all instinctually."

LEFT With the continuing vitality of Mexico's indigenous craftspeople, modern reinterpretations of traditional decorative effects have little need to lapse into "folksy" mimicry. Interior designer Armand Aubery was able to furnish the interiors of the Hacienda de San Antonio with a variety of contemporary South American arts and crafts. This richly decorated living room features a carved Guatemalan wall hanging and Mexican cabinets decorated with wood and bone inlay.

ABOVE Richly embellished artifacts in the Hacienda de San Antonio bear witness to the popularity of baroque exuberance in Spain and its former colonies. The Mexican artist Jesus Guerrero Santos made this highly distinctive silver mirror frame and the flanking pair of candelabra.

A LAKESIDE HOUSE

JOSE DE YTURBE IS an influential contemporary Mexican architect whose ideals remain close to those of Luis Barragán, the man rightly credited with helping to reclaim Mexican architecture from what has been widely perceived as the overly austere influence of the Modernists during the first half of the 20th century.

Yturbe's recently built family home, in the highly desirable resort of Valle de Bravo, is a strikingly beautiful residence, set against the dramatic backdrop of a mountain range and offering an enticing prospect across the tranquil waters of a large inland lake. It also benefits substantially from a temperate microclimate that practically demands an outdoor living and dining area.

The house itself, constructed of adobe-covered masonry walls and roughly curved pine columns, supports a tiled roof characteristic of the regional architecture. Inside, the design is dominated by natural wood, white walls, and terracotta floors, against which vivid bursts of color are presented in often surprising ways. Bright geraniums in terracotta pots cast a mottled blush on white walls; serried ranks of glass jars are filled with luminous bright liquids; and patterns of light shift beneath the fretwork of overhead glazing. Elsewhere, strong color is used to create spatial effects or express moods. All these effects take place within a setting of calm, considered restraint. The understated demarcations of internal space are typical: an open-plan living room leads directly into a kitchen, while a change of level and a low stuccoed balustrade are all that mark the boundary of the dining room.

The lasting impressions of Yturbe's lakeside house are not only that the traditional Mexican love of color endures, but also that an important lesson has been learned from the Modernists: with color, as with other things, what you leave out is as important as what you put in.

TOP RIGHT & ABOVE An arrangement of geraniums and liquid-filled jars, beneath a glazed roof, makes reference to South American pyramids. Yturbe's cool, spare interiors provide a neutral setting for his adventures with color, while a minimalist stairway evokes the geometry of an ancient *ziggurat*.

FAR LEFT This covered outdoor living–dining area mediates between the interior and exterior of Yturbe's lakeside house. The roof provides shade from summer sun and shelter in the rainy season, while the encroaching vegetation forms an intrinsic part of the decor.

ABOVE Reflected light is a constantly changing element in Yturbe's interior. His plain white walls often act as screens onto which sunlight, shade, and reflected color are projected in natural response to the daily movement of the sun. The overall effect is carefully calculated, and the results infinitely varied.

RIGHT The chromatic intensity of the colored liquids in the glass demijohns changes not only with the contours of the containers, but also in response to the darker tones of their potted geranium neighbors. The result is a multiplicity of reds, and an effect reminiscent of "glazing" in watercolor painting, where rich color is gradually built up by overlaying translucent layers of pigment.

LAS ALAMANDAS

HALFWAY BETWEEN Puerto Vallarta and Manzanillo in Jalisco, Mexico, the exclusive resort of Las Alamandas lies in the sort of natural paradise that for once does justice to the hyperbole of the travel writer. At the resort's center is a hotel comprising four *casitas* with eleven suites, all filled with Mexican arts and crafts. The dazzling beauty of the surrounding palms, beaches, surf, and lush vegetation is such that one might expect a hotel to have difficulty making any visual impact at all. In fact, the Las Alamandas complex (named after the yellow alamandas flower) – which was conceived by the late Gabriel Nuñes, completed by Manuel Mestre, and is now owned by Isabel Goldsmith – is a striking collection of buildings that take the use of color in Mexican architecture to dramatic new levels.

Palm trees and a yellow mosaic path lead via a fountain to *casitas* that are much influenced by hacienda-style decor

and architecture. Tiled floors, thick rendered walls, shuttered windows, and high vaulted ceilings set the tone, but it is brilliant color that undoubtedly makes the most impact. Typical of the complex, the beachfront Casa del Domo, with its vibrant orange and pink exterior, is decorated in the traditional way: paint is first applied and then ragged in a process that needs to be repeated every few months in order to maintain the color's brilliant richness. Similarly, vibrant primary colors are often used on the risers of steps. Both functional and decorative, steps are a recurring architectural feature of Mexican architecture and figure heavily in the geometry of Las Alamandas.

ABOVE Mexican architect Luis Barragán (1902–88) pioneered the use of color in 20th-century Mexican architecture, employing it as a tool to highlight a space or define an area. His influence is clearly evident in the Casa del Domo at Las Alamandas, where strong, vivid pink and orange-ocher hues are used to enhance the bold architectural forms of a curved wall and cupola.

LEFT Vegetation plays an important decorative role in Mexican architecture. Here, verdant palms shade the entrance to a *casita* at Las Alamandas, and mediate sunlight over its facade, creating random patterns and gradations of tone in the paint.

FAR LEFT An extensive range of blues, including cerulean and ultramarine, is used in Mexican decoration. Traditionally symbolic of the sea and sky (as well as peace and truth), blues were widely employed by early Mesoamerican civilizations, notably the Toltecs. They remain in vogue in Pacific coastal resorts such as Las Alamandas, where they provide an appropriate visual link with the ocean.

LEFT Natural wood tones also make a significant contribution to the decorative palette at Las Alamandas. Here, the supporting log pillars, rafters, and purlins of a terrace roof are cut from local wood and left exposed in traditional hacienda style.

LEFT While subtle gradations of color, created by ragging, can be seen in the exterior paintwork on this breakfast terrace, more structured pattern is introduced in the floor, which has been laid with stone tiles and volcanic pebbles. The glazed earthenware on the breakfast table was designed by Gorki Gonzales in Guanajuato; the flowers are the yellow alamandas from which the hotel complex gets its name.

ABOVE The vernacular building traditions of the region are acknowledged in the steeply pitched thatched roofs, known locally as *palapas*, that cover some of the terraces. Made from palm fronds, they provide protection from rain and shade from the sun, and also have a cooling effect on the occupants by allowing heat to rise away from the floor of the terrace.

LEFT Palm fronds contribute to an unforced composition of natural green grading into applied orange ocher and Mexican pink.

RIGHT Flights of steps were an architectural staple in the earliest Mesoamerican period, when they were often used as much for decorative and dramatic effect as for their practical purpose. At Las Alamandas, too, functional steps take on a decorative role with the addition of colors that come straight from the candy store and Mexican marketplace.

BELOW A Mexican *equipal* chair stands next to a wall featuring the classic color combination of *rosa Mexicana* and yellow. The color juxtaposition derives from two indigenous forms of vegetation: the sunflower and bougainvillea, a tropical plant known for its brilliantly colored pink and red bracts.

FAR LEFT An approach to the Las Alamandas complex, featuring plants in pink-painted terracotta tubs, an ocher and gray-black geometric-pattern mosaic path, and an avenue of shady palms.

ABOVE LEFT Daylight filters through a log canopy onto a daybed – a demonstration of the architect's predilection for blurring the visual boundaries between exterior and interior. Architectural features such as the stone window frames and the bed-surround are picked out in green against a background of orange and natural wood tones.

LEFT The view from a living area through the entrance hall to the main front door. The glazed architraves are picked out against white in *rosa Mexicana*. As on the terrace opposite, the floor is covered with glazed earthenware tiles, which are laid in a bold geometric pattern of alternating hexagonal and diamond shapes.

Las Alamandas is sited on a 1,500-acre (600-hectare) beachfront tract of land that once belonged to Bolivian "Tin King" Antenor Patiño, who also developed the Las Hadas resort in the nearby town of Manzanillo. When Patiño died, he left the fertile land to his granddaughter, Isabel. It was her simple strategy – to conserve the surrounding landscape and keep the complex small – that determined the high quality of the buildings. This scaled-down hacienda approach affects everything from the treatment of the building fabric to the nature of the furniture, most of which is made on the premises. Local vernacular styles predominate, as seen in the brightly cushioned *equipal* chairs from Colima, pottery from San Miguel de Allende, and colorful Guatemalan pillows.

As is so often the case with Mexican buildings, the link between natural surroundings and buildings is accentuated not only by familiar structural elements such as patios, but also by color and light. At Las Alamandas the fronds of palms outside and the fingers of light penetrating the interiors through windows and slatted roofs find constant echoes in one another. This may be a modern luxury resort, but its visual manners make it part of Mexico's architectural tradition in a way that is never nostalgic, simply apt.

"Color is a complement to architecture. It can be used to widen or enclose a space. It is also imperative for adding that touch of magic to an area."

(Luis Barragán, architect)

LEFT The terrace of Casa del Domo at Las Alamandas overlooks tropical, palm-studded gardens. Its walls are ragged a strong orange terracotta and a particularly vivid pink – colors that serve to define the architectural form of the building. Like the pink, purple, orange, red, yellow, green, and blue of the upholstery fabrics, they are inspired by the fruits, flowers, toys, and clothes of a typical Mexican marketplace.

RANCHO LA PEÑA

This page Externally, the visual impact of Rancho La Peña is achieved by an extremely bold use of strong, flat, textured slabs of complementary color. The sunlight etches dark, shifting shadows into the recesses and rabbets between the blocks and planes. Architectural quotations from the past include the stylized *ojo de buey* (bull's-eye) perforation (below), recalled by architect Manuel Mestre from early colonial hacienda grain-storage buildings.

THE RANCHO LA PEÑA was designed and built in the mid-1990s by Manuel Mestre, an architect adept at translating traditional Mexican colors and forms into contemporary design. Located in the Valle de Bravo, at the end of the Sierra Madre, the house typifies Mestre's fondness for creating individual spaces embellished with reworked architectural details from Mexico's past. Texture is as important as color to this architect. The ranch is built of earth-and-mud bricks reinforced with special straw and, in the larger expanses, rendered with concrete. Wooden structures have been added to the building to fulfill the expectation of seeing wood in a ranch building, and some internal surfaces are textured with woven mats placed on wet cement prior to painting.

Mestre's preoccupation with texture and mixed materials results in rich blend of surfaces and finishes, inlays and laminates: terracotta floor tiling features a wooden pegged pattern, while a chimneypiece is made of nailed bronze sheets. Even so, the primary impact of Rancho La Peña is the potency of its colored surfaces. Mestre mixes the pigments himself and, as the architect, makes all the

color decisions. The result in this case is an exceptionally resonant palette dominated by green inside and a daring interplay of red and green surfaces outside.

Built for a wealthy client, the ranch has a generous complement of rooms and outdoor activity spaces: swimming pool, tennis court and, of course, an outdoor dining terrace, with overhanging roof. Color control extends outdoors, too, with geraniums in terracotta tubs picking up the colorful drama of the building's exterior. The external upper section of the main building is particularly dramatic in its use of striking complementary colors set off by a bold geometric organization of blocks and planes. It is as if Mestre has not only borrowed the toy-bright palette of the nursery, but taken the child's building blocks for inspiration, too.

In many respects, Rancho La Peña can be seen as a virtual museum of Mexican decorative effects in architecture. From the tiniest inlaid stones to bold polychromatic walls descended from distant haciendas, this is a celebratory home for which the past is not an ideal, but a glorious repository of shimmering effects.

THIS PAGE Inside the main house, the palette darkens to a vibrant but nevertheless restful green, offset against white and punctuated by natural-colored wooden furniture and structural fixtures. The Mexican love of stepped effects is pushed to new extremes, with pebble-and-mortar inlaid stairs and even "deconstructed" steps.

FOLLOWING PAGES A view over the swimming pool, across the garden and an orchard of peach trees flanked by pine forests, to the Sierre Madre in the distance.

Using the Mexican palette

Traditional and contemporary Mexican decoration is mainly characterized by a palette of strong and bright colors inspired by the sun, moon, and sky; by native Mexican soils and clays; and by indigenous trees, shrubs, fruits, and flowers. The botanical references are many and varied, with the colors of azaleas, bougainvillea, pansies, sunflowers, yellow alamandas, and cacti making a contribution to the palette, alongside those of bananas, mangoes, papayas, and tamarind pulp. Many of the characteristic Mexican color combinations – notably pink with orange or yellow, or orange with blue or green – are visually very striking, and may even seem shocking to northern eyes familiar with more muted tones. Nevertheless, architects and designers rarely employ them for purely picturesque effect. Indeed, like the equally popular but less flamboyant combinations of white with blue, green, or pink, these colors are almost invariably used to serve an architectural purpose: to adjust the visual temperature; to widen or enclose a space; or to define particular fixtures. Whether it is in a traditional or modern setting, the overall effect of the Mexican palette is to enhance the dramatic qualities of the architecture.

ABOVE Complementary colors used in close proximity tend to enhance each other's purity or chromatic intensity – as illustrated by this juxtaposition of pale green and orange. The effect is reinforced here by the intense blue of the Mexican sky, which enhances the orange.

RIGHT Reddish-brown earth colors are key components of Mexican architecture. In this instance, earthy tones are contrasted with the cool whiteness of the adjoining walls, establishing a strong sense of form and space.

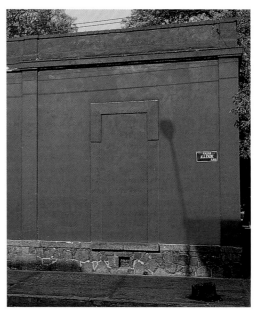

ABOVE Large expanses of blue, combined with terracotta and wood tones, further cool shaded areas.

LEFT & BELOW Strongly contrasted colors help define architectural features.

BELOW The use of mud bricks, terracotta tiles, and burnt orange and pale green render helps link this ranch to the landscape.

RIGHT The distinctive pink known as *rosa Mexicana* is usually employed against earth colors, yellow or, as in these doorways, white.

PAINT LIBRARY
Stellenbosch Oak

JOHN OLIVER
Hot Sahara

JOHN OLIVER
Kinky Pink

LEFT & ABOVE Matte earth colors, because of the way they absorb light, display wide variations of tone, depending on whether they are subject to strong sunlight or shade. This quality allows architectural configurations to be defined within an otherwise monochromatic color scheme.

BELOW Saturated ocher, orange, and pinkish-red make a powerful color combination and create a hothouse atmosphere in this entrance area. The colors work particularly well with the profusion of green foliage, while the cool stone floor helps prevent the ensemble from becoming overpowering.

DULUX COLOUR SELECTOR
Rich Red

FIRED EARTH/
PAINT PORTFOLIO
Better Class Red

BRATS LTD
MEDITERRANEAN PALETTE
Tuscany • 107

LEFT Vivid yellow walls reflect both light and warmth into a stairway.

BELOW Shadows cast by oak beams onto white walls enhance the dramatic quality of the architecture.

CROWN EXPRESSIONS
Fresh Cypress • FC– 8

DULUX COLOUR SELECTOR
Simply Indigo

CROWN COLOUR PLANNER
Moonshine

Moroccan style

RIGHT The internal courtyard of the Hotel Villa Maroc in Essaouira. The hotel comprises three 18th-century French-designed houses that have been sensitively restored to preserve their original features and revive their authentic color schemes. The blue-painted balustrade and door frame provide visual relief from the cooling whitewashed walls and columns. The water-based blue paint, known as *bleu entre mer*, is made in Casablanca.

RIGHT La Maison Arabe is a 19th-century mansion in the medina (old town) of Marrakesh and now a hotel. In an exotically decorated internal courtyard, the octagonal columns supporting the first-floor gallery are painted yellow-ocher, and given a cracked-varnish finish to resemble marble. The pierced fretwork balustrade above is a traditional Moroccan design. The tables, stools, and chairs are painted majorelle blue.

ABOVE An archway in the colonnaded internal courtyard of Dâr Zellij, a restored 18th-century townhouse in Marrakesh. The underside of the arch is embellished with *tagguebbast* (sculpted plasterwork) painted in earthy reds, browns, and blue.

JUST AS the imagination of the French artists Eugène Delacroix and Henri Matisse was fired by the imagery and colors of Morocco during the 19th and the early 20th centuries, so numerous designers from overseas have subsequently found inspiration in the architecture, ornament, and decorative palette of this exotic North African country. Indeed, over the last 30 years, many of these designers, working mostly for an influx of French, English, and American expatriate residents, have fueled the restoration of countless old Moroccan houses, and in doing so have also helped promote the revival of a number of traditional decorative techniques indigenous to the region.

A history of international trade, occupation, and colonial rule has insured diverse architectural influences over the centuries, particularly in the cities of Tangier, Rabat, Casablanca, Essaouira, Marrakesh, and Agadir. The Romans, Spanish, and English all left their mark. Nevertheless, it is the French influence, dating from the 18th century and flourishing under their protectorate rule from 1912 to 1956, that remains most evident today. The French legacy is not, however, a crude imposition of Western architecture, but rather a sympathetic blend of European and North African designs that rapidly evolved into a distinctive Moroccan style. The explanation for this partly resides in the French leaving the old medinas (town centers), with their narrow streets, bustling souks (markets), and traditional *riyâds* (Arab townhouses with enclosed, colonnaded courtyards and gardens), largely untouched. But it is also due to the fact that many of the Classical Revival and Art Deco townhouses designed by French architects incorporated decorative features derived from the native Arab and Berber vocabularies of ornament. For example, in addition to the adoption of features such as the *wast ad-dar* (enclosed central courtyard), surfaces were often extensively sheathed in intricately patterned *zouak*

ABOVE Also at Dâr Zellij, this 18th-century *bab* (battened-plank door) is decorated with a locally made water-based blue paint. The streaking and mottling evident in the finish is the result of exposure to strong sunlight over the passage of time.

ABOVE The large double doors leading off the central courtyard at Dâr Zellij feature monochromatic radiating star patterns in *zouak* work, a traditional Moroccan technique of painting on wood.

ABOVE These mosaic wall panels at Dâr Zellij are known as *zelliges*. The pattern of linked geometric shapes radiating out from a central star is a traditional design known as *testir* (the Prophet's spider web). The colors are typically Moroccan.

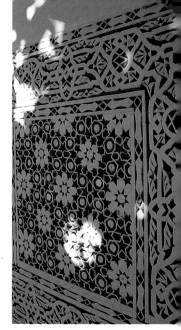

ABOVE & TOP The top-floor gallery of a small house *(douiriya)* annexed to La Maison Arabe has pale terracotta floor tiles and whitewashed walls. The upper sections of the walls, like the ceiling, are decorated with intricately sculpted *tagguebbast*.

LEFT The central courtyard at Dár Zellij is typical of 18th- and 19th-century townhouses in the medina of Marrakesh. The white and pale terracotta color scheme is carried over to the orange trees, which have been whitewashed to discourage insects.

(painted woodwork), *tagguebbast* (sculpted plasterwork), and *zelliges* (mosaic tilework), or coated with *tadelakt* (a smooth, marblelike finish made from sand and quicklime). Over and above these decorative features, however, it was the French use of the distinctive North African color palette that underpinned the fusion of styles.

Much of the inspiration for the palette and, indeed, the source of many of the pigments and constructional materials, is derived from the sands and soils of Morocco, which range from various shades of yellow, ocher and

umber, to pink – the latter being particularly prevalent around Marrakesh. In addition to black, and the ubiquitous, cooling white, other hues popular in Morocco include pale and dark blue, purple, orange, and numerous tints and shades of green. Often highly luminous, and mostly inspired by the fertile gardens that proliferate in Moroccan courtyards, these colors also have secular and religious significance: white, for example, is the color of Paradise; red represents fire, blood, and the Moroccan national flag; while green is the color of Islam.

ABOVE Majorelle blue-painted chairs and tables are sited at intervals behind the colonnades of the central courtyard at La Maison Arabe (see main picture on page 192). The carved and pierced wooden panels are framed by carved and painted *tabiya* blind arches. *Tabiya* is a plasterlike compound made from quicklime and the local pink sand, giving it a pinkish-red hue.

RIGHT Pinkish tones derived from the sands of Marrakesh are also evident in this bathroom at Dâr Zellij. The ceiling is a variation of the traditional Moroccan technique of *tataoui*, in which eucalyptus and oleander withies are laid at right angles across rafters of trimmed branches. Here, small branches are used instead of the withies and have been lightly whitewashed to produce a light and airy finish.

DÂR TAMSNA

SET IN EXTENSIVE grounds, and comprising two large houses – Maison Nakhil and Maison Ouardaia – and a small cottage, Dâr Tamsna was purchased in a dilapidated condition in 1987 by Meryanne and Gary Loum-Martin. The style in which they refurbished the buildings and gardens as a luxury hotel was inspired by their love of ethnic North African interiors, by the work of Moroccan architects Charles Boccara and Elie Mouyal, and by the location: the Palmeraie (date-palm oasis) of Marrakesh.

Founded c.1062–70 as a fortified town, by Youssef bin Tachfine, Marrakesh was described in the 16th century by Frenchman Louis de Marmol as "a great city, the best in all Africa." The intervening years have done nothing to diminish its majestic beauty. A cosmopolitan city, lying low on a plain with the snow-capped Atlas Mountains towering in the distance, Marrakesh is surrounded by 4½ miles (7 kilometers) of rose-red colored walls. Built around 1126, they gave they gave the city its other name, "El Amara" (the red), and are made from tabiya, a

compound of the highly distinctive, local pinkish-red sand strengthened with quicklime. Both tabiya and pisé – another traditional Moroccan building material, made from sun-dried earth reinforced with lime or straw, and much used by the influential modern architect Elie Mouyal – have been incorporated in the reconstruction of Dâr Tamsna, and their presence serves to integrate its exterior with the indigenous architecture of the region.

The homogenous relationship that the Loum-Martins were intent on establishing between Dâr Tamsna and its location is further underpinned by the use of a local marble – marbre d'Ifrane – as a flooring material in most of the rooms, and by the application of tadelakt to many of the walls. A compound of sand, quicklime, and earth-colored pigments, tadelakt was originally used to line the interior walls of Moroccan hammams (steam baths), but since the 1970s has enjoyed a notable revival in residential interiors. Its method of application – it is smoothed and polished with soft stones and then washed

ABOVE The walls of a living room in the Maison Nakhil are decorated with *tadelakt* pigmented in a tobacco color. The paler sandstone fireplace is carved with a traditional honeycomb pattern and stylized floral motifs. The pink-upholstered sofas were made by a local carpenter.

RIGHT Also at Maison Nakhil, this verandalike structure is inspired by a *bhou* – an area traditionally used in Moroccan houses to sit in and look out over the garden. Under a white ceiling, its walls and columns are coated with tobacco-color *tadelakt* inscribed with a geometric-pattern frieze.

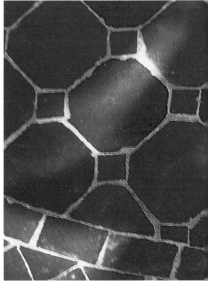

ABOVE & BELOW Since pre-Roman times, mosaic tile work known as *zillij* has been a significant source of color and pattern in North African architecture. Applied to floors, walls, and, as here, tabletops, the *zelliges* (tiles) are cut into simple geometric shapes and laid in patterns that have changed little over the centuries. Polychrome tiles accentuate the complexity of a pattern; monochrome tiles such as these simplify and embolden it.

with olive oil soap, prior to a final waxing – is a lengthy and labor-intensive process. Nevertheless, the lustrous finish – which can range from dark brown, through pinkish-red, to a pale tobacco hue, depending on which pigments and types of sand are used – is substantially less expensive than marble cladding or leather lining, the opulent finishes that *tadelakt* most closely resembles.

Moroccan architectural and decorative traditions are also evident at Dâr Tamsna in numerous other fixtures. Notable examples in some of the drawing rooms include intricately patterned off-white, *tagguebbast* (sculpted plaster) friezes, and compartmented ("coffered") ceilings made of cedar wood. The latter, like the cedar-wood window frames, shutters, and fretwork screens employed throughout the houses, were made by local craftsmen, and

LEFT The walls and fireplace of a living room in Maison Nakhil are coated with *tadelakt*. The complementary-colored ceiling is made of cedar wood, and compartmented in a traditional Moroccan design. The pottery on the mantelpiece and the table under the wall-mirror (made from an old window frame) are local. The *kelim* and the throw on the footstool display colors and geometric patterns and motifs characteristic of North Africa.

ABOVE To create a vacation feel, a matte-finish, water-based yellow paint – made in Marrakesh – was chosen for the walls of one of the bedrooms in Maison Ouardaia. The octagonal table was bought in the local souk (market) and is decorated with panels of *zouak* work (painting on wood). The Marrakesh souk was also the source of the yellow-ocher-colored glazed-earthenware vase and the table lamp with delicately pierced brass shade.

their mid-brown, natural wood tones blend harmoniously with the colors of the *tadelakt*.

The warm, earth-colored palette that dominates the decoration of many of the rooms is also echoed in their furnishings and decorative artifacts. Prominent examples include pinkish-red upholstered sofas; brown, red, and ivory-colored *zouak* (painted wooden) chests and tables; burnt-umber and yellow-ocher earthenware vases; dark-patinated, pierced bronze and copper lamps; and striped, polychromatic flat-weave *kelims* (rugs). Sourced mostly

ABOVE The main bedroom at Maison Nakhil is floored with panels of variegated off-white and black North African marbles. The walls are coated with *tadelakt* and topped with an off-white *tagguebbast* (sculpted plaster) frieze.

"…Marrakesh is the great market of the south; and the south means not

ABOVE The other end of the main bedroom (shown on page 197) at Maison Nakhil. The *tadelakt* wall finish here has a richer and more reddish tone than that in some of the other rooms of Dâr Tamsna. It also has a more lustrous quality – achieved by extensive polishing with stones, washing with olive-oil soap, and waxing. Combined with the subtle mottling and gradations of color across its surface, this gives a marblelike appearance that echoes the room's real marble floor. The white cotton drapes and bed linen, and pastel-striped bedcover, add an airy touch.

LEFT A rich, reddish-terracotta-colored *tadelakt* finish has also been applied to the walls of this connecting bathroom at Maison Nakhil. To unify the decorative scheme, it has been carried over to the encasement paneling around the bathtub. The window frame and the doors of the vanity have been painted a matching color. The white-enamel tub and washbasins, together with the ivory-colored towels, have an important role to play in cooling and lightening the interior, while the large cedar-framed wall-mirror enhances the natural light from the window and increases the sense of space.

BELOW The color schemes in the north-facing bedrooms at Maison Ouardaia are primarily white or green or, as here, a balance of the two. White and green is a cooling combination, especially when the room is exposed to northern light.

LEFT Apart from the polychrome floor mosaic, decoration of the staircase landing at Maison Ouardaia is confined to white, pale beige and umber-stained woodwork. These neutral colors help define the architectural components of a distinctly Modernist-inspired interior.

BELOW Also at Ouardaia, an antique chest from the Atlas Mountains displays traditional painted *zouak*-work patterns.

only the Atlas, but all that lies beyond…" (Edith Wharton, novelist, 1927)

from Berber craftsmen working in the local souks, many of whom are direct descendents of the city's first inhabitants, these pieces provide another close tie between Dâr Tamsna and Marrakesh, both past and present.

Another important consideration for the Loum-Martins when decorating the interiors was their desire to enhance the sense of light and space. On the stairs and landings this was achieved by employing colors such as pale pink and beige on the walls, and white on the flat-plaster ceilings. White was also chosen for the ceilings in many of the rooms where *tadelakt* was used. In this context the white not only visually increases the height of the rooms, and helps to reflect natural and artificial light around them, but also has a cooling effect by counterbalancing the intrinsic warmth of the earth-colored wall finishes.

In some of the bedrooms, white ceilings have been combined with flat-painted yellow or green walls. Yellow with white was chosen as a particularly bright and sunny

combination. Green and white were chosen not only for their aesthetic qualities, but also for symbolic reasons. In Islamic culture, white represents paradise, and is considered a very positive color. Green is the color of the Prophet Muhammad's banner and is thus traditionally used as an expression of attachment to the teachings of Islam. Moreover, green represents growth and renewal, and so establishes a significant link between Dâr Tamsna and its verdant gardens, which thrive in Marrakesh's well-irrigated, fertile Palmeraie. The close relationship between house and garden, however, is not only the result of the symbolism or coordination of specific colors, nor of the names chosen for the houses (Nakhil means rose, and Ouardaia palm tree). Inspired by the work of Moroccan architect Charles Boccara, the Loum-Martins added a number of terraces and veranda-like structures that physically extend the houses into the outdoors and, in so doing, blur the boundaries between the interior and exterior.

ABOVE Six-pointed stars and flower heads are recurring motifs in North African mosaics. Red, the color of the Moroccan flag, features prominently in this floor mosaic at Dâr Tamsna.

Using the Moroccan palette

Cooling whites and off-whites, together with warm sand and soil colors such as gold, yellow-ocher, sandstone, beige, pinkish-red and umber, dominate the Moroccan palette, especially in wall finishes. An extensive vocabulary of greens (a color symbolic of Islam) is also employed, as are tones of blue, ranging from light to dark, muted to vibrant. Other prominent hues, apart from black, include bright yellows and pinks, and strong reds and purples. These appear mainly in the patterns of tilework, painted furniture, and upholstery fabrics and, like the greens, are largely inspired by the colors of Moroccan orchards and gardens.

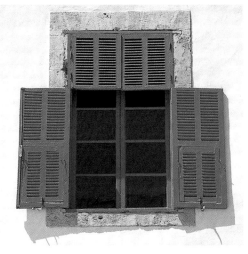

LEFT In addition to the chromatically intense, darker "Majorelle" blues, lighter blue tones and more muted, less reflective shades are also in evidence. Here, contrasting tones help to distinguish the different forms of wooden fixtures.

BELOW A wide range of green is employed in Moroccan decoration. Almond-green is notable among the lighter tones; darker shades include "astral" green and olive-greens that verge on black.

ABOVE Strong, vibrant blues are often used in Moroccan decoration, mostly for doors, shutters, and tilework. They became particularly fashionable in the 1920s, when the French painter and designer Louis Majorelle made extensive use of them in his Marrakesh villa.

RIGHT Cooling whites are also popular, sometimes contrasted with the earth colors of stone and brick, or the natural tones of indigenous wood.

LEFT In Moroccan decoration, blue and yellow are often used in close proximity. Being broadly complementary – rather than discordant – colors, they tend to enhance each other's chromatic intensity, or color saturation. As with these Majorelle-blue wooden shutters and adjacent yellow-ocher stone window frame, set against neutral white walls, the result is a vibrant composition that stimulates rather than overpowers the eye.

LEFT The definition given to different architectural components by the use of varying tints is even more marked when contrasting colors are used. Here, arched door- and window-frames of sandstone are clearly defined against whitewashed walls. Similarly, the door and window-frames are picked out from their surrounds in majorelle blue and, in turn, the glazing bars of their fanlights are highlighted in white.

BELOW The color scheme of this sitting room at La Maison Arabe is inspired by the traditional colors of the *souks* (the old markets) of Marrakesh, and balances coolness and warmth. Cool colors in the white ceiling, the blues of the upholstery fabrics, and the tiles of the fire-surround contrast with the sponged wall finish, the terracotta-tiled floor and the red, pink, and yellow flat-weave *kelim*.

DULUX COLOUR SELECTOR
Biscuit

CROWN EXPRESSIONS
Mustard Spice · MS–4

DULUX COLOUR SELECTOR
Golden Dazzle

RALPH LAUREN PAINT
SANTA FE COLLECTION
Mesa Sunrise · SF12B

RALPH LAUREN PAINT
SANTA FE COLLECTION
Rodeo Red · SF18A

PAINT MAGIC/
JOCASTA INNES
Rue Green

DULUX COLOUR SELECTOR
Azure Oasis

CROWN EXPRESSIONS
Blue Mosel · BM–10

ACE ILLUMINATIONS
Ocean Park · 25–A

Shaker style

LEFT Unlike the Amish, the Shakers did not reject the benefits of new technology. Nor was their practical approach limited to the crafting of natural materials. At the Church Family Dwelling in Hancock, Massachusetts, a cast-iron stove demands a chimney; rather than perforate the ceiling, the flue pipe takes the shortest route to the outside. Apart from the wood tones of the oiled furniture, color is restricted to the blue-painted woodwork, and is contrasted with whitewashed flat plaster walls and ceiling.

ABOVE The Shaker ladderback chair was designed to be hung on the wall when cleaning. But that was not its only innovation: its feet often contained a clever softwood ball-and-socket device to protect floors and provide square, stable contact at any angle. The design of the large bureau seen here is also typically Shaker. Eschewing fancy veneers, its plain surfaces are made of solid oiled hardwood.

S HAKER STYLE IS UNIQUE in that it grew out of an austere view of the world that had very little time for style at all. In fact, Shaker style was characterized by an absence of style – if the word is understood to be about form and decorative embellishment rather than substance. The Shakers – even more than the Modernists (see pp. 130–35), whom they predated by well over a century – believed implicitly that form should follow function and that design should emerge unforced from appropriate manufacturing techniques. Unlike the Modernists, however, some of whom held overbearing opinions about architecture and society in general, the Shakers treated the creation of their environments and artifacts as byproducts – as natural extensions of their chosen way of life – and saw the process of creating them as a form of prayer.

The Shaker way of life and its aesthetic was to succeed only after the most daunting of beginnings. In the mid-18th century, a splinter group of radical English Quakers adopted the practice of shaking, shouting, dancing, whirling, and singing in tongues – hence the "Shaking Quakers," or Shakers. Ann Lee, or "Mother Ann," an illiterate textile worker from Manchester, England, became their leading light and the author of a Shaker doctrine that was eventually to flourish in the US Following her conversion to the Shaker sect in 1758, she became a zealot in the fullest sense of the word. She was repeatedly persecuted and imprisoned by the state for taking part in boisterous religious services, and she later claimed to have witnessed a series of revelations that persuaded her that she was the female side of God's dual nature and the second incarnation of Christ. In what seems a particularly shortsighted strategy for future growth, Ann Lee established celibacy as a cardinal principle of the Shaker sect; then in 1774, to avoid further persecution, she crossed the Atlantic. At this period, various religious sects flourished

ABOVE Absence of clutter and simplicity of decoration are keynotes of Shaker interiors. In these rooms at the Church Family Dwelling in Hancock, the decorative palette is largely restricted to neutral white and two colors: the mellow brown of the wooden floorboards, and the dark blue of the painted doors and architraves. The only decorative flourish is the rust-red-painted baseboard in the far room.

LEFT This open-string winding staircase at the Church Family Dwelling in Hancock exemplifies the simplicity of line and symmetry of proportion that characterize Shaker architecture. Its fluid, elegant form is a product of specific engineering demands, while its decoration – oiled wooden treads and handrail, and green-painted stringers, risers, and balusters – serves only to emphasize its sweeping lines and harmoniously integrate it with the floorboards and woodwork of the stairwell.

ABOVE The window and baseboard in this corner of a Shaker bedroom are painted a shade of yellow-ocher that is echoed in the natural wood tones. The sliding sash window is characteristically undraped.

side-by-side in the USA and were more or less tolerated. If the portents were not good, the eventual outcome was little short of miraculous.

Despite some initial persecution in the US, Ann Lee and her small band of followers managed to settle in Niskeyuna (now Watervliet), New York, a region that was at the time sympathetic to revivalism. Within five years, the Shakers had made several thousand converts among the locals. After Ann Lee's death in 1784, a new leader took over the sect, one who was to introduce the communal ethos that would come to define Shaker values and, in the process, give the United States a native design idiom that owed nothing to Europe or anywhere else.

Under the leadership of Elder Joseph Meacham and Eldress Lucy Wright, the first Shaker community was established in 1787 at New Lebanon, New York. This center led a movement that subsequently spread through New England and out west into Kentucky, Ohio, and Indiana. By 1826, there were eighteen Shaker villages in eight states; most were prosperous communities running model farms and conducting business with outsiders in an exemplary fashion.

If all societies get the architecture they deserve, the same can be said of the Shakers' small societal network of communities. The buildings and the artifacts that grew out of their way of life were spare, naturally elegant, and frequently ingenious. The "style" of the Shakers perhaps finds a parallel in the "style" of well-made industrial machinery or specialized professional tools. It is the sort of unconscious style where the forces of physics, the existence of special needs, and the principle of truth to materials are all distilled into the sort of design that has no need of surface styling. Everything in the Shaker communities, from meeting house to simple chair, was fashioned stringently to serve its intended use, and nothing more. All superfluous decoration, such as inlays and moldings, was eliminated.

A certain sense of celebration, even pleasure, came from creating such objects, and was essentially derived from the philosophy of manual work as a form of prayer. However, there was also an undoubted sense of satisfaction to be had from the sheer ingenuity of some impressive inventions. From screw propellers and turbine waterwheels to the clothes pin, Shaker design was highly innovative, but of course it was only ever undertaken in response to the needs of the community.

The enticing possibilities of color seem to have tested the Shakers' principles of austerity from time to time. Although their "decorative" palette was most usually

determined by the materials they used – that is, largely defined by the colors of the natural world: wood, leather, straw, and stone, or perhaps homemade bricks – livelier colors were gradually introduced. By the first half of the 19th century, Shaker style had matured, and furniture, window shutters, and other architectural fixtures would from time to time be painted in grayed reds, blues, yellows, and greens. Similarly, nesting wooden storage boxes might come in contrasting, grayed primaries; yarn was dyed a variety of hues not always strictly necessary to its purpose; and barns and houses, once painted tan for reasons of

ABOVE Pattern is rarely, if ever, applied in Shaker interiors. The random figuring of the marble slab under the stove is intrinsic to the stone, and the rectilinear division of walls, doors, and floors is simply a product of their construction – albeit emphasized by the rather austere blue and white color scheme.

LEFT The enduring popularity of Shaker style is witnessed by the construction of an imitation Shaker village in Sagaponack, Long Island, New York. Architects Deamer–Phillips and interior designers Carlson Chase have captured the simplicity of the style in this living room, which features finely crafted built-in storage furniture and is dominated by the colors and textures of natural materials.

BELOW The light and airy ambience of this Sagaponack bedroom is similarly grounded in the Shaker tradition. The over-stuffed chair cushion and large double bed are unlikely to have met with approval, however.

cost, were increasingly decorated in the expensive white paint that had formerly been reserved exclusively for the community meeting house. Shaker society had become comfortable, but the concessions that its visual manners made to prosperity amounted to little more than a sparing application of the more muted colors from the American Colonial palette (see pp.36–53).

Today, the vanished world of the Shakers is to be glimpsed only in museum villages such as Hancock, Massachusetts, or museums such as Fruitlands, at Harvard. However, Shaker style has endured in later 20th-century developments such as the imitation Shaker village at Sagaponack, Long Island, and in the current fashion (on both sides of the Atlantic) for reproduction Shaker furniture and artifacts. Moreover, unlike the sect that created it, Shaker style will undoubtedly continue to be influential beyond its time. The plain colors and the fitness-to-purpose principle espoused by the Shakers do not date easily. Indeed, harmonious austerity would seem almost to guarantee perennial popularity.

Shaker Revival is therefore not so much any single reprise of an historical fashion, but more a continuous living relationship with something timeless. Of course,

what was conceived in a spirit of frank simplicity can sometimes look to the modern eye like calculated minimalism. But this was never the case: above all, the original Shaker style was innocent, never contrived. In a Post-Modern design world of historical quotation, pastiche, and even parody, it is perhaps this fundamental quality that remains its greatest appeal.

BELOW Despite a degree of internal architectural complexity that belies the Shaker model, the sense of space and the unifying color scheme – white and natural wood tones – in this dining room and sequestered kitchen at Sagaponack evoke the original Shaker spirit of "fitness for purpose."

Using the Shaker palette

The early Shaker palette was founded on neutral whites and creams, and the natural colors that were inherent in their basic building and furnishing materials – namely, wood, stone, leather, iron, and brick. In due course, relatively brighter colors were introduced for painted wooden fixtures, for furniture, and for artifacts such as nesting boxes. These colors were generally confined to the more muted or "grayed" shades of red, yellow, blue, and green that had found favor in American Colonial interiors (see pp.36–53), and were always used sparingly: it is extremely rare to find more than two or three colors employed in one room.

LEFT The decorative convention of using two tones of the same basic color to define subtly the various architectural features of a room was often employed in Shaker houses. Here, a very pale tint of the green paint used on the woodwork and built-in furniture has been applied to the walls. Bolder contrasts of color are restricted to the drawer knobs and wall pegs – all of which are picked out in blackish-brown against the green background.

ABOVE The color scheme in this stairwell reinforces the form of the fixtures. Set against whitewashed walls, the woodwork is presented in two harmonious hues: vegetal green, and the yellow-brown tones of an indigenous hardwood.

RIGHT As in the stairwell, color is used in this attic room to define the basic structural components: whitewash for the plaster walls, and a Shaker mid-blue for the woodwork.

ABOVE The natural figuring and grain of wood, and its warm yellow-brown tones, are core components of the Shaker look. So, too, is the quality of construction, simplicity of line, and fitness-for-purpose that are much in evidence here.

LEFT Re-creations of the Shaker look inevitably incorporate concessions to comfort that would have had no place in an original Shaker house. The overall design and palette, however, remain true to the style.

SHAKER LTD
Cabinetmaker's Blue

SHAKER LTD
Wild Bayberry

J.W. BOLLOM & CO. LTD
NATURAL COLOR SYSTEM
S 6030–B70G

SHAKER LTD
Soldier Blue

ABOVE The paints on this Shaker door and frame would once have been evenly opaque; the streaking is caused by fugitive pigments breaking down through exposure to light. The effect can be simulated by dragging freshly applied wet paint, and rubbing it back with sandpaper when dry.

ABOVE RIGHT, RIGHT & FAR RIGHT Whitewashed walls boldly contrasted with blue- or yellow-ocher-painted woodwork enhance the strong rectilinear emphasis of Shaker architecture.

SHAKER LTD
Antique Yellow

J.W. BOLLOM & CO. LTD
NATURAL COLOR SYSTEM
S 3040–Y30R

DULUX COLOUR SELECTOR
Natural Terracotta

LEFT Even the Shakers could not resist creating objects of beauty where duller things would have proved just as useful. The elegant swallow tail joints of these nesting boxes may be functional, and the *en escalier* formation might be a visual mnemonic about Shakers climbing the steps of heaven. However, the Shakers' use of blue, red, and yellow tones of paint to decorate them must surely be an exceptional example of art for art's sake.

J.W. BOLLOM & CO. LTD
NATURAL COLOR SYSTEM
S 4040–Y40R

SHAKER LTD
British Red

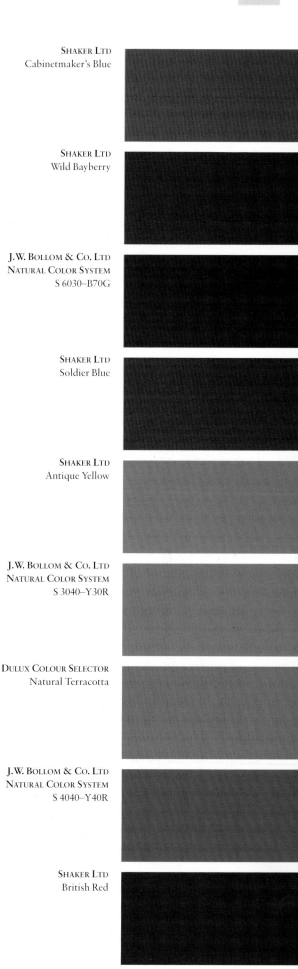

CHAPTER 4

The Predominant Colors

ABOVE Blue distemper paint – in paler tints and darker shades – covers the walls and furniture in a room at Regnaholm, a Swedish Gustavian manor house that dates to the 1760s.

LEFT A cascade of glass demijohns, filled with red liquid and alternated with geraniums in terracotta pots, at the Valle de Bravo home of Mexican architect José de Yturbe.

FAR LEFT A selection of mineral and vegetable pigments in the studio of Italian painter Giugi Maria Sesti at Castello di Argiano, near Siena. They include *rosso cinabro*, *terre verde*, *giallo limone*, and *cobaltone*.

Understanding color

OUR PERCEPTION OF COLOR is subjective, and our reactions to color are therefore variable and hard to define. Touching on aesthetic and psychological issues as well as styles and fashions, the act of experiencing color can be described, but not always analyzed. The color spectrum itself, however, does have some intrinsic qualities that can be fairly easily summarized. The discussion here refers exclusively to subtractive colors – the process whereby paints or dyes are mixed. Additive color, where beams of light are combined, as on a TV screen or computer monitor, behaves quite differently.

Any color can be said to have three basic characteristics. **Hue** distinguishes between different colors: red, yellow, blue, or whatever. **Chromatic intensity** describes the level of saturation: a brilliant red mixed with black or white becomes duller and less intense. **Tonal value** measures how reflective a color appears and is an indication of how light or dark it is.

The relationship between colors is usefully displayed on a color wheel like the one shown opposite. The basic categories are as follows. The **primary colors** are red, blue, and yellow. In theory, all other colors can be mixed from these, although in practice it often results in an unacceptable loss of chromatic intensity and tonal strength. **Secondary colors** are those produced by mixing two primaries. **Tertiary colors** are those produced by mixing a primary and a secondary color.

There are also two other subdivisions relating to a color's tonal value: a **tint**, produced by adding white to make a color lighter; and a **shade**, created by adding black to make it darker.

When choosing a color, bear in mind that its appearance will always be modified by the presence of another color. There are no hard and fast rules, but note that in close proximity **complementary colors** – opposites on the color wheel – heighten each other's saturation to create vibrant contrasts. Also, **discordant colors** tend to be those with common characteristics, such as vivid pink and maroon, which are both derived from red. One discordant color can be used discreetly to accent another, but if both are employed in close proximity on a large scale they will almost always clash.

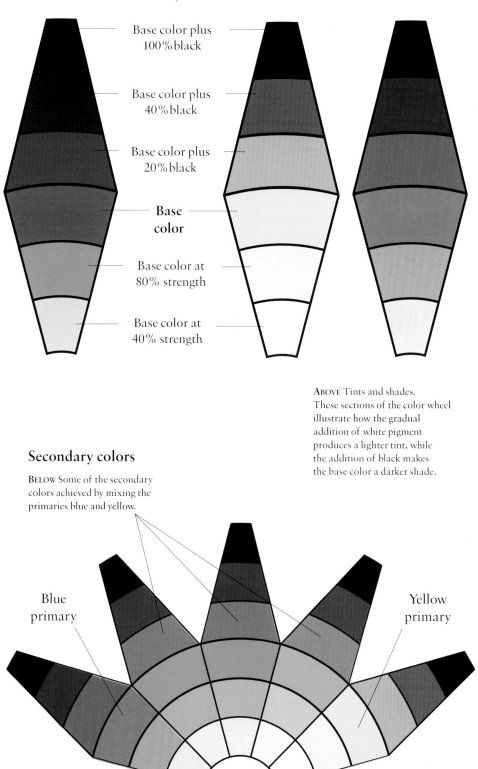

Primary colors

Base color plus 100% black

Base color plus 40% black

Base color plus 20% black

Base color

Base color at 80% strength

Base color at 40% strength

ABOVE Tints and shades. These sections of the color wheel illustrate how the gradual addition of white pigment produces a lighter tint, while the addition of black makes the base color a darker shade.

Secondary colors

BELOW Some of the secondary colors achieved by mixing the primaries blue and yellow.

Blue primary

Yellow primary

The color sphere of twelve representative colors

RIGHT A color wheel made up of the three primary colors – red, yellow, and blue – and a series of secondary colors created by mixing any two primaries. Complementary colors are shown directly opposite each other. The progressive effects of tint and shade move outward from the center of the wheel.

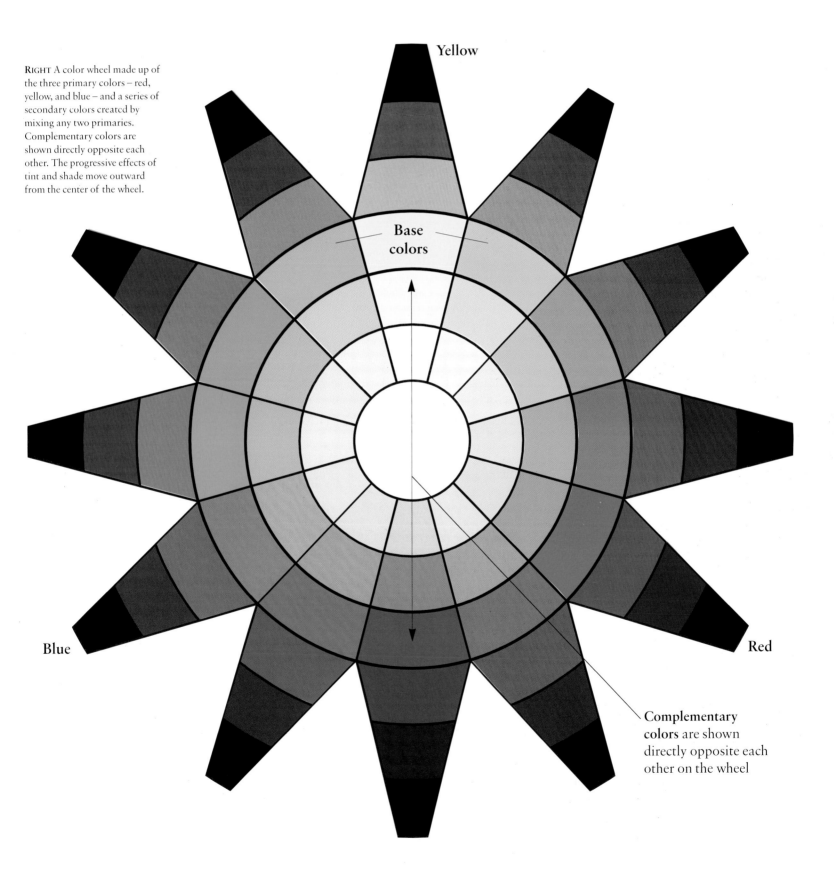

Yellow

Base colors

Blue

Red

Complementary colors are shown directly opposite each other on the wheel

DULUX COLOUR SELECTOR
Sexy Pink

RALPH LAUREN PAINT
SANTA FE COLLECTION
Arroyo Pink · SF02C

ACE ILLUMINATIONS
Carlyle · 53–E

RALPH LAUREN PAINT
SANTA FE COLLECTION
Sedona Pink · SF13D

SANDERSON SPECTRUM
Cerise Pink · 18–12D

CROWN EXPRESSIONS
Brasserie · BR–8

ACE ILLUMINATIONS
Tulip Time · 53–A

J.W. BOLLOM & CO. LTD
NATURAL COLOR SYSTEM
S 2050–R30B

DULUX HERITAGE COLOURS
GEORGIAN (1714–1837)
DH Blossom

Reds

C ONCEPTS OF COLOR are not universal, and the feelings we may associate with a given color cannot be taken for granted in other cultures. Indeed, not all languages have a word for green, blue, yellow, or orange. All languages have a word for red, however, which is the most commonly encountered color after black and white. With its overtones of lifeblood and excitement, red seems to be the most vibrant and stimulating of colors. In spite of – or perhaps because of – its connotations of anger and danger, red it is seen as a powerful life-affirming color. Red does not always need to appear in its most saturated form to generate a positive response in the viewer. Strong pink and rich brown take on vibrancy from the red base hue, while the dramatic juxtaposition of red and white is often intensified if the red is not too strong – perhaps because the use of a saturated red and pure white together can be visually rather jarring.

ABOVE At a casita in Jalisco, Mexico, *rosa Mexicana* niches, door and window frames, flowers, and upholstery are contrasted with white plaster walls.
LEFT In an 18th-century French salon, original off-white painted *boiseries* provide the backdrop for new pastel-pink drapes.
RIGHT The stuccoed walls of a 19th-century Spanish Colonial house in Mexico City are painted a deep terracotta-red hue.
FAR RIGHT In a Mexican interior by José de Yturbe, a stone fountain fronts pink "Aztec" steps and rows of red geraniums in terracotta pots.

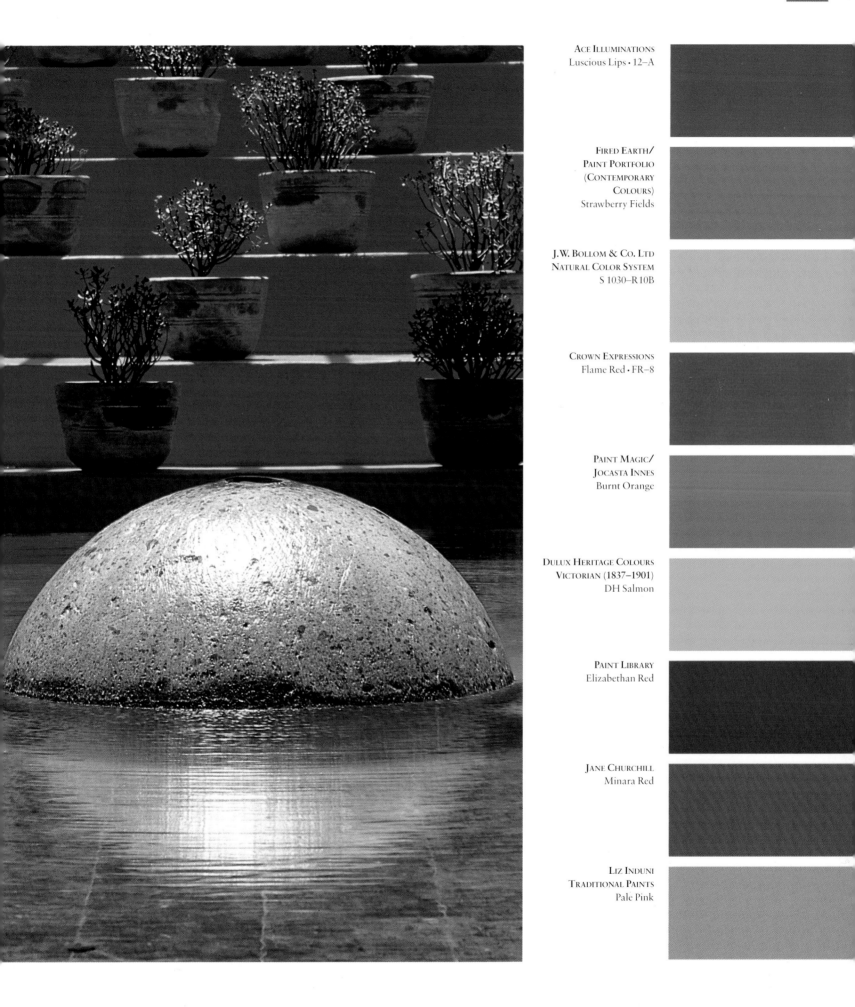

ACE ILLUMINATIONS
Luscious Lips • 12–A

FIRED EARTH/
PAINT PORTFOLIO
(CONTEMPORARY
COLOURS)
Strawberry Fields

J.W. BOLLOM & CO. LTD
NATURAL COLOR SYSTEM
S 1030–R10B

CROWN EXPRESSIONS
Flame Red • FR–8

PAINT MAGIC/
JOCASTA INNES
Burnt Orange

DULUX HERITAGE COLOURS
VICTORIAN (1837–1901)
DH Salmon

PAINT LIBRARY
Elizabethan Red

JANE CHURCHILL
Minara Red

LIZ INDUNI
TRADITIONAL PAINTS
Pale Pink

Yellows

LACKING THE MORE UNIVERSAL associations that red possesses, yellow can still make a very powerful decorative statement. For many people, warm yellow can just be as uplifting as strong red. However, large expanses of certain shades of yellow tinged with blue may result in an unattractive, somewhat bilious effect. When it is used as an accent color within a lower-key decorative scheme, yellow can almost always provide a brilliant highlight, but large expanses of the color need to be carefully judged because it can be overpowering in confined spaces.

Yellow, for obvious reasons, evokes the sun – witness the stylized radiating yellow symbol that features in many children's paintings. Van Gogh's endlessly reproduced sunflowers provided the 20th century with a potent icon of fierce natural vitality and yellow's key association is one of sunlight and wellbeing.

There is a broader perception that yellow, along with orange and red, is a "warm" color, while blue and green are "cold." This has practical ramifications when it comes to decorating interiors. You will often find that in order to achieve the same sensation – or illusion – of warmth, a "cool" room painted pale blue will be given a higher thermostat setting than a "warm" room decorated in a yellow or pale orange. Our expectations can strongly condition what we see, creating a combined response – but one that is no less "real" for the fact of being based upon an optical illusion.

ABOVE Yellow dominates this early 19th-century interior at the Palacio Real de Aranjuez. The silk damask wall hangings, gilt moldings, and finely figured walnut table all pick up the yellow of the walls.
RIGHT The drawing-room walls in an early 19th-century villa in south London are flat-painted saturated yellow, characteristic of the Regency style.
FAR RIGHT At the "Ministry of Taste" in Marrakesh, the luminous yellow of the courtyard walls is broken by the browns of the columns, balustrade, and stickwork.

J.W. Bollom & Co. Ltd
EMULSION STAINERS
Yellow Chrome

PAINT LIBRARY
Orlando

CROWN COLOUR
COLLECTION
Cream Silk

DULUX HERITAGE COLOURS
Lemon Colour

J.W. Bollom & Co. Ltd
NATURAL COLOR SYSTEM
S 1050–Y10R

ROSE OF JERICHO
Yellow

DULUX COLOUR SELECTOR
Apricot Crush

SANDERSON SPECTRUM
Sun Buff Lt • 8–20M

ACE ILLUMINATIONS
Sahara • 86–E

CROWN EXPRESSIONS
Bahama Blue • BB–8

CROWN EXPRESSIONS
Winter Lake • WL–4

CROWN EXPRESSIONS
Oxford Blue • OB–3

ACE ILLUMINATIONS
New River Gorge • 26–B

CROWN COLOUR
COLLECTION
Blue Mosel

SANDERSON SPECTRUM
Blue Day Lt • 24–14P

DULUX COLOUR SELECTOR
Blue Lagoon

ROSE OF JERICHO
Ultramarine Blue

CROWN COLOUR
COLLECTION
Dewberry Frost

Blues

B LUE SEEMS TO ATTRACT a large number of colloquial qualifiers in English, with sky blue, navy blue, powder blue, and royal blue being just a few of the variations of this versatile hue. The color of smoke, vapor, and distant hills, blue is most commonly associated with the sky and water; this no doubt helps give it its strong "elemental" quality. One of the playful uses of deep sky blue is as a ground for decorative clouds or stars. The concourse ceiling of Grand Central Station in New York City features gold constellations and signs of the zodiac on what was once an inky blue night firmament, but which renovation has now revealed to be a lively turquoise.

In more conventional decorative use, blue is often thought to encourage a restful, cool ambiance, particularly in its lighter shades. However, at its greatest saturation, blue can also be one of the sharpest, most incisive of colors. The purples and mauves that derive from it are often associated with rich ceremony and royal trappings, while in certain countries purple takes the place of black (or in some cultures, white) as the color of mourning. However, the perceived coolness of blue does little to explain the widespread use of "the blues" to describe a mood of sadness.

ABOVE Solid planes of different blues in a Post-Modern London house.
RIGHT A floral paper with gray-blue ground at the Morris-Jumel Mansion, New York.
FAR RIGHT A high-gloss blue, enlivened with gold motifs, in a North American Victorian home.
BELOW Lilac- and lavender-blue in an Arts and Crafts-style house in Pasadena, California.

J.W. BOLLOM & CO. LTD
NATURAL COLOR SYSTEM
S 4050–R50B

ACE ILLUMINATIONS
Ruth's Best • 16–A

SANDERSON SPECTRUM
Elegance • 21–11M

DULUX COLOUR SELECTOR
Real Indigo

SANDERSON SPECTRUM
Rajah • 23–6D

SANDERSON SPECTRUM
Purple Petal • 23–10M

ACE ILLUMINATIONS
Viking King • 58–A

RALPH LAUREN PAINTS
SANTA FE COLLECTION
Canyon Iris • SF11D

DULUX HERITAGE COLOURS
DH Lilac

SANDERSON SPECTRUM
Emerald · 55–15U

DULUX COLOUR SELECTOR
Terrific Turquoise

PAINT LIBRARY
Constantia Blue

DULUX HERITAGE COLOURS
VICTORIAN (1837–1901)
Victorian 21

DULUX COLOUR SELECTOR
Soft Willow

CROWN COLOUR COLLECTION
Swiss Chalet

CROWN EXPRESSIONS
Castaway · CA–6

RALPH LAUREN PAINT
CANYON ROAD COLLECTION
Summer Sod · CR03C

J.W. BOLLOM & CO. LTD
NATURAL COLOR SYSTEM
S 1010–B90G

Greens

GREEN – THE COLOR OF MONEY, the color of envy…? Not necessarily. These are not universally understood phrases because of different international perceptions and associations. American banknotes may be green, but most other countries' paper money is not. "Green with envy" does not necessarily translate felicitously into languages other than English. However, there is one almost universal connotation for green – its association with plants and trees. This was dramatically reinforced in the final decades of the 20th century with the growth of "green" environmental awareness, and the color has become an international emblem for movements and products focused upon moral, political, and social attitudes toward the natural world. Of course, from the acanthus of the Corinthian capital through Botticelli to Art Deco, the green-leaf decorative device has always had potent natural associations, but as our relationship with the natural world is re-examined in the context of contemporary living, these traditional associations with renewal, growth, and natural vegetation have been strengthened.

Green, particularly in its lighter tints, also evokes restfulness and harmony – providing an antidote to man-made finishes and industrial colors. However, a strong green with a bias toward blue can be more racy and intense, on a par with electric purples and reds where a bold use of saturated color suggests daring and adventure. In its lightest tints, green is usually considered a particularly restful alternative to pure white. In certain contexts, the bright, bluish green of verdigris can be deployed to suggest the attractive aging of a variety of materials and surfaces.

ABOVE Softwood *boiseries* in the principal dining room of a restored mid-18th-century French chateau have been flat-painted Veronese green by the architectural historian and designer Andrew Allfree. The color is echoed in the verdigris-hued drops and swags of an 18th-century French candelabrum.
LEFT In a late 17th-century manoir in the Lot-et-Garonne region of France, fielded-panel doors from the 18th century have been repainted flat, saturated mid-green, a popular contemporary color for woodwork in rural French interiors.
FAR LEFT The vibrant hues of indigenous Mexican vegetation provided architect Manuel Mestre with the inspiration for the green-painted walls at the Rancho la Peña in Mexico's Valle de Bravo. These are harmoniously combined with a palette of natural earth and wood tones typically found in locally produced tiles, pots, and furniture.

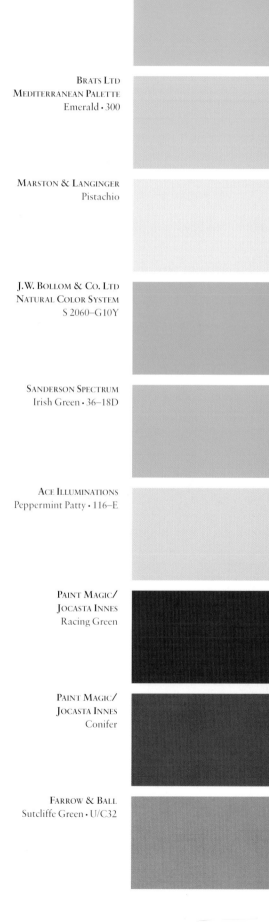

ACE ILLUMINATIONS
Apple Green • 37–A

BRATS LTD
MEDITERRANEAN PALETTE
Emerald • 300

MARSTON & LANGINGER
Pistachio

J.W. BOLLOM & CO. LTD
NATURAL COLOR SYSTEM
S 2060–G10Y

SANDERSON SPECTRUM
Irish Green • 36–18D

ACE ILLUMINATIONS
Peppermint Patty • 116–E

PAINT MAGIC/
JOCASTA INNES
Racing Green

PAINT MAGIC/
JOCASTA INNES
Conifer

FARROW & BALL
Sutcliffe Green • U/C32

CHAPTER

5

Traditional Sources of Color

ABOVE The walls of an outbuilding in Montalcino, Italy, are decorated with a paint containing the locally sourced pigment *terra rossa di Argiano*.

LEFT The window frames and shutters of a French farmhouse are decorated and preserved against insect infestation with a limewash that has been pigmented with woad.

FAR LEFT *Isatis tinctoria* growing in southwest France. Its flowers and leaves are the source of woad – a blue pigment described in the 17th century as *bleu de Roi* ("King's blue").

Earth pigments – terra rossa

LIKE NUMEROUS FORMS of vegetable matter (see woad, pp.226–9), pigments derived from earth rich in iron oxides are one of the oldest sources of color for artists and decorators – their use has been dated to prehistoric times. Because of their resistance to lime, these inorganic earth pigments were employed in *buon* (or "true") fresco work – the most durable method of painting murals, whereby the pigments are completely fused with a damp plaster ground to become an integral part of the wall surface. While no *buon* frescoes have survived from ancient Greece, historically important examples can be seen in excavated Pompeiian villas of the 1st century A.D.; in earlier Chinese tombs at Liao-yang, Manchuria; and in caves at Ajanta in India that were decorated in the 6th century A.D. Some of the finest *buon* frescoes were executed in Italy during the Renaissance, most notably by Michelangelo and Raphael in, respectively, the Sistine Chapel and the Stanze of the Vatican, in Rome. In addition to these highly decorative examples, earth pigments have also provided a readily accessible and relatively inexpensive means of coloring the various water- and oil-based paint media used to decorate exterior and interior plaster and wooden surfaces of ordinary houses.

The three most commonly found and used earth pigments are classified as follows: ochers, the colorant property of which is solely iron oxide, and which tend to occupy the yellow part of the color spectrum; siennas, which range from yellowish brown to reddish orange, and contain 30–75 percent iron oxide; and umbers, which have a high manganese dioxide content and are generally brown in color. All these pigments can also be calcinated (heated to a high temperature) to make them richer and darker, in which state they are respectively referred to as burnt ocher, burnt sienna, and burnt umber.

Other notable earth pigments include the various reds – sometimes referred to as red ochers – that are produced from iron-oxide hematite ores such as Spanish oxide and Persian Gulf oxide; black from magnetite; yellow from limonite; brown from siderite; and dark brown from pyrites. In addition to these naturally occurring examples, various synthetic iron-oxide pigments have also been produced. Two prominent examples are the iron-oxide reds – ranging from light Turkey red to dark Indian reds – created by calcinating ferrous sulfate; and what is usually referred to as Venetian red, which is obtained by calcinating ferrous sulfate in the presence of lime.

ABOVE LEFT & RIGHT Guigi Maria Sesti excavates a seam of the mineral pigment *terra rossa di Argiano*. Italy is rich in minerals (especially red iron oxides) and thus for thousands of years has been a major source of earth pigments for artists and decorators alike. Before they can be used to color paint media (see opposite), earth pigments are subjected to a process of refining that removes the extraneous mineral and vegetable matter contained in the soil.

THIS PAGE The first stage of the refining process is to place the dry soil in a bucket and soak it in water for three or four days. Once the lumps of soil that contain the mineral deposits have been softened with water, they are transferred to a wide-meshed box sifter and pounded with a pestle to break them down into smaller lumps. These fall through the mesh into an earthenware container and any large stones are left behind in the sifter. The process of breaking down and sifting the soil containing the mineral deposits is repeated several times with various hammers. When it has been reduced to a coarse, damp powder, it is transferred to a bucket and mixed with water again to form a slightly lumpy, creamlike consistency. This mixture is transferred to a fine-mesh box sifter and, using a spatula, further refined through the sifter into another container.

THIS PAGE More water is added to aid the process of refining the *terra rossa di Argiano* pigment through a fine-mesh sifter. This process can be repeated a number of times. Once all remaining small lumps have been removed, the pigment is left to dry to a very fine powder. It can then be used to color various types of paint. It can be added to limewash (see right and far right), a highly durable mixture of lime putty, water, and raw linseed oil; or mixed with milk of figs to produce a water-soluble paint suitable for wood and plaster surfaces. Guigi Maria Sesti has also used the pigment to make egg tempera, by mixing it with linseed oil, water, and egg yolk.

Traditionally, earth pigments are usually, although not exclusively, named after the location from which they are derived. Because it is a major source of iron-oxide-rich earths, Italy has figured large in this labeling process. Thus siennas are named after the city of Siena, umbers after the region of Umbria, and Verona green (or *terre verte*) after the city of Verona (not to be confused with the chrome-based, emerald-colored Veronese green named after the 16th-century Italian artist, Paolo Veronese).

While the vast majority of earth pigments were first dug or mined centuries ago, new discoveries still occur. The illustrations on these pages show a recent example unearthed in the late 1990s by the Italian fresco-painter and winemaker Guigi Maria Sesti who, together with his wife Sarah, owns the small village of Argiano, near Montalcino and Siena. Discovered during the excavation of one of his fields, the small iron-oxide-rich seam has yielded a distinctive reddish-brown pigment. Using a centuries-old process, the pigment is ground down and eventually refined into a dry powder. The color can be used in a variety of ways. Here, Sesti uses it in a water-based medium to paint the walls of a building. In keeping with tradition, the pigment takes its name – *terra rossa di Argiano* – from the village it comes from.

THIS PAGE Guigi Maria Sesti applies the *terra rossa di Argiano* paint to the rendered walls of a building in Argiano. As it dries, it is absorbed into the surface of the render – a process that consolidates the durability of the finish. There are also aesthetic advantages: paints derived from local soils and clays create a visual link between a building and the surrounding countryside.

Vegetable pigments – woad

FAR LEFT Near Toulouse in southwestern France the source of woad – *Isatis tinctoria* – shows yellow in the field. This is the first stage of a labour-intensive process, and a chromatic transition from a yellowish-green via the greenish-blue that will eventually result in the distinctive blue pigment.

LEFT Once the leaves of the plant have been harvested, they are soaked and stirred in water. During this procees, which takes around four hours, the water begins to take on a greenish hue. At the same time, the woad pigment is beginning to form – but at this stage it is transparent.

ALONGSIDE earth pigments (see pp.222–5), various forms of vegetable matter provided the primary means of coloring paints and fabrics prior to the invention, in the mid-19th century, of synthetic aniline dyes. Notable examples include madder, a red pigment derived from the root of the plant *Rubia tinctorum*; quercitron, extracted from the inner bark of a species of oak to create various yellows; indigo, a blue pigment drawn from the leaves of the plant genus *Indigofera*; and woad. The latter, which like indigo is also a blue pigment, is among the oldest – it has been used since the Stone Age – and has proved to be one of the most versatile and durable.

Prepared from the leaves of *Isatis tinctoria*, a biennial plant native to southern Europe, woad has been credited with many properties beyond that of a pigment or dye. Its purported healing powers have led to it being applied as a compound to wounds and even used as the basic ingredient of a draft to settle the stomach. However, it has been most consistently prized for its decorative qualities. For example, the blue sections of the Bayeux Tapestry dyed with woad have remained virtually unfaded for almost a millennium – an enduring testament to the quality and

permanence of the pigment. Woad was also very highly prized in Renaissance Europe, when it was known as *bleu de Roi* ("King's blue"), and during the 17th century, when it was in widespread use as both a paint pigment and a fabric dye. At this time around 30–40,000 tons were exported each year to London, Antwerp, and Hamburg from Toulouse in southern France – a lucrative trade that brought considerable prosperity to the city and the surrounding countryside.

The traditional method for preparing woad took nine to twelve months, and began with hand-picking the leaves and then crushing them to a pulp in a circular stone woad mill, which was driven by mules or horses. The pulp was then made into balls, known as *cocagnes*, which were laid on covered trays to dry. After drying, the balls were crushed to a powder in the same mill and then taken to the floor of a couching house, where they were wetted and turned to encourage fermentation. The mass was turned daily and wetted again for a period of up to nine weeks. This process took considerable skill, since the dye can be destroyed if too much heat is generated during fermentation. The resulting blue compost was then put into barrels and shipped to the fabric dyers.

RIGHT The liquid is drained off and transferred to an oxidation tank where air is pumped through it. As a result of oxygen exposure, the pigment develops opacity and changes color.

FAR RIGHT ABOVE Initially, the pigment takes on a yellowish hue, followed by green and then, as tested on this sheet of cotton fabric, a pale bluish-green.

FAR RIGHT BELOW Here, the final chromatic transition, from bluish green to blue, is nearing completion.

The two types of paint – oil- and water-based – made from woad can then be created by mixing the residue in the woad dyers' tanks with, respectively, turpentine and oil (such as linseed), or limewash. The latter mixture, which had inherent insect-repellent properties, was traditionally applied to wood and plaster, the oil-based paint being usually confined to finer wooden surfaces.

Although, for reasons of cost, woad was gradually superseded by indigo from the late 17th century on, and by synthetic indigo from the mid-19th century, it has enjoyed a revival in recent years. This has been fueled by companies such as Bleu de Lectoure in France (whose premises are shown on these pages), who have improved traditional methods of production, and by a renewed appreciation of woad's aesthetic qualities. Ranging from a light, delicate blue to a strong, dark indigo blue, but always containing a hint of gray that adds sophistication, woad has convincingly been dubbed the only blue that ages with nobility and beauty.

FAR LEFT Once the oxidation process has been completed, the liquid will be transferred to a "resting" tank where it will be left overnight to deposit itself at the bottom. It is then filtered off, refined, refiltered, and dried to form a powder known as "blue gold".

BELOW Today, woad pigment is in demand as a dye for fabrics and fibers such as cotton, silk, linen, and, as here, cashmere. Extremely stable, it can be diluted to produce an infinite variety of blue tints and shades.

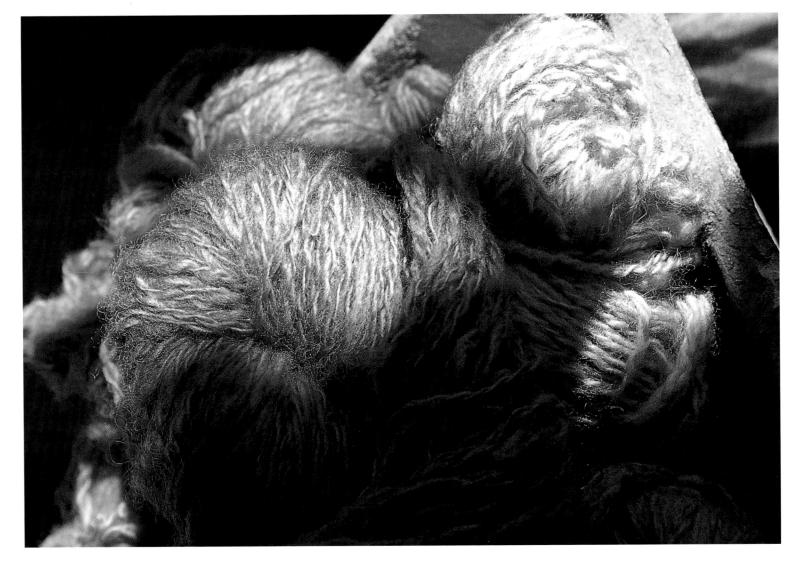

ABOVE & RIGHT The woad pigment can be mixed with oil and turpentine to produce a highly durable oil-based paint (for wood), or with limewash to create a more translucent and insect-repellent colorwash (for wooden or plaster surfaces). The woad-painted shutters and door seen here are on the premises of the Bleu de Lectoure company. They are a distinctive feature of rural houses in Le Pays de Cocagne in southwestern France, a region named after the balls of pulped *Isatis tinctoria* leaves produced in the early stages of traditional woad-making.

Glossary

A

acanthus Foliage ornament styled on the leaves of the *Acanthus spinosus* plant, native to the Mediterranean.

Adam style A Neoclassical style after Scottish architect Robert Adam in the late 18th century – see pp.70–3.

adobe Sun-dried, as opposed to kiln-baked, brick. Used for house building in Mexico and the Southwest.

aegricane Head or skull of a ram or goat, sometimes used in *swags or *festoons in Greco-Roman ornament.

Aesthetic movement A late 19th-century English and American movement reacting against the eclecticism and "excessive clutter" of *High Victorian style. A precursor to *Art Nouveau, it reflected a strong Japanese influence and overlapped with the *Arts and Crafts Movement.

anthemion A floral motif styled on either the flower of the *acanthus or the flower and leaf of the honeysuckle.

Apolline Form of decoration derived from Greco-Roman art and comprising representations or symbols of the god Apollo, whose attributes were time, poetry, and music.

arabesques Stylized interlaced foliage patterns of Near Eastern origin, first used in European ornament and decoration from the mid-16th century.

arcading A series of linked arches supported by columns.

architrave Collective term for the moldings surrounding a window, door, panel, or niche.

Art Deco A style of decoration and ornament popular in the 1920s and '30s. Primarily characterized by geometric and abstract forms, such as stepped shapes, sun motifs, and emblems suggestive of speed and dynamism.

Art Nouveau A style of decoration characterized by sinuous curves and flowing lines, asymmetry, and flower and leaf motifs. Prevalent from the late 1880s to 1914, especially in Europe.

Arts and Crafts movement Initiated in Britain in the 1860s, influential on both sides of the Atlantic until the 1930s. A reaction to the poor quality of mass-produced goods following the Industrial Revolution, it advocated a return to traditional methods of craftsmanship.

ashlar Square blocks of stone masonry.

Aztec One of the dominant civilizations in Mexico prior to the Spanish conquest.

B

baize Coarse woolen cloth used mainly as table covering.

Bakelite A synthetic, plasticlike resin with a high chemical and electrical resistance.

balusters Small posts in rows supporting a handrail, together forming a balustrade for a staircase or terrace.

balustrade see *balusters

banquette French term for a low-seated settee.

Baroque A style of architecture popular in Europe in the 17th century. Inspired by Classical precedents and characterized by elaborate, sculptural forms and motifs.

barrel vault An arched vault or ceiling in tunnel form, either semicircular or semielliptical in profile.

bas-relief A form of sculpture in which the figures or images stand slightly away from the background material (usually stone or plaster) from which they are sculpted.

baseboard The wooden board placed around the base of an internal wall at the junction with the floor.

battened-plank door A door made of vertical wooden planks nailed to horizontal strips at the back, sometimes with diagonal braces or "double-boarding" in which planks rather than battens are used on the reverse.

Bauhaus ("Building House") An arts and crafts school founded in Germany in 1919 that emphasized the importance of unifying design and function. The school was closed in 1933 because it offended Nazi Party views.

Berbers One of the Muslim peoples of North Africa.

bergère French upholstered wing armchair with a rounded back and wide seat, with caned or upholstered sides, first made in the early 18th century.

Biedermeier A style of decoration and furniture popular in Austria and Germany *c.*1818–60. Influenced by *Empire and *Regency styles and characterized by *Neoclassical forms and use of fine hardwood veneers.

block-printing A printing technique that involves applying dye or ink to a relief carving on a wooden block. The image is then transferred to the chosen surface by pressing the block onto it by hand.

boiseries French term for wooden wall paneling decorated with carvings and/or moldings.

bolection molding A C- or D-shaped profile molding. Popular on paneling in the late 17th and 18th centuries.

brocade A heavy silk fabric with a raised pattern that is often highlighted with gold or silver thread.

broken pediment A *pediment with a gap in the crown, sometimes filled with an urn or similar decoration.

Brussels carpet A flat-woven carpet with looped uncut pile. Usually woven in two or three colors.

bunting Strings of flags or pennants.

butt-jointing A method of laying boards in which their flat sides are pressed or "butted" against one another.

C

cabriole leg A curving leg modeled on the hind leg of an animal that tapers in toward the foot. Used on tables and chairs from the late 17th century on.

calcium carbonate The main component of lime, chalk, and gypsum.

candlewick A tufted cotton fabric used for bedspreads.

cantilevered A method of supporting a horizontal projection, such as a step(s), balcony, beam, or canopy, by a beam or beams held at one end only – usually through the wall into which the end is keyed.

capital The top or head of a column or *pilaster.

Capodimonte An Italian ceramics factory located near Naples from 1743–9. Known for its soft-paste porcelain.

carbon A nonmetallic element in the form of graphite or diamond.

cartouche A decorative panel comprising a round, oval, or scroll-shaped frame with a plain or decorated center.

casement A window frame hinged on one side so it swings out or in to open.

casita Mexican term for a villa (also a bathroom).

chaise longue French term for an upholstered, elongated chair, often called a day bed.

checked pattern A "counterchange" pattern of regularly spaced squares of two or more alternating colors.

chesterfield A heavily padded sofa.

cheval A large mirror hung in a frame and designed to swivel in it.

chevrons V-shape motifs for water and lightning.

chinoiserie Western interpretations of Chinese furnishings, artefacts, and styles of ornament.

chintz A printed cotton with a polished finish.

chromatic intensity A measurement of how *saturated or pure a color is and to what degree it has been diminished by white, black, or other colors.

chrysocolla A copper-based green pigment.

clapboard Overlapping wooden boards (weatherboards) forming the external covering of a wood-framed house.

coat-of-arms *Heraldic insignia derived from knights' coats worn over chain mail.

cobalt A metallic element from which the blue pigment cobalt blue is derived.

coffered ceiling A ceiling divided into compartments (coffers) by exposed beams or by plaster moldings.

Colonial Revival see pp.48–51

Colonial style see pp.36–9

compartmented Alternative term for *coffered.

complementary colors Colors that in close proximity heighten each other's *chromatic intensity.

Corinthian One of the most ornate Classical *Orders.

cornice A plain or decorative molding used to cover the edge between the walls and the ceiling.

cotton twill Fabric with woven diagonal lines or ridges.

Craftsman style An holistic style of house-building in the U.S. in the early 20th century, in which houses were designed as harmonious units. Typified by high-quality woodwork and the use of beautiful woods.

craquelure The fine network of cracks or crazing that can occur over time in the surface of paints or varnishes.

cresting A decorative border on a wall, roof, or screen.

crockets Leaf carvings employed in Gothic architecture.

cupola The internal part of a dome or a concave ceiling.

curule A camp-stool shaped chair with curved legs originally used by Roman magistrates.

cyphers Interlaced initials.

D

dado Lower section of a wall, running from floor to approximately waist height, where it is often defined by a wooden or plaster molding (a dado rail).

damask A fabric first produced in Damascus in the 4th century A.D. and made in the West from the 15th century. True damasks are monochrome with patterns created by the contrast between a shiny ground and matte figuring.

Delftware Dutch and English earthenwares covered with a white tin-glaze then decorated with a design, generally in blue. Originated in the Dutch town of Delft.

dentils Decorative molding made up of regularly spaced "toothlike" blocks. Originally applied as a cornice, but from the 17th century also applied to furniture.

diaper patterns Geometric patterns (such as *trellis-work), often embellished with motifs and imagery.

dimity A white cotton fabric woven with a stripe pattern.

Directoire The period 1795–99 when France was ruled by the Directoire. Also the severe, pared-down style of Neoclassicism fashionable in France at that time.

discordant colors Colors that when used in close proximity "clash" or simply do not work well together.

distemper A primitive, opaque paint made from whiting or chalk dissolved in water and bound with animal glue.

documentary fabric An exact replica of an historic fabric. If any element is altered, it is a reproduction.

dormer window A small window with a *gable projecting from a sloping roof.

drab A brownish-grayish-green paint color particularly popular during the first half of the 18th century.

duchesse French term for a *chaise longue with a rounded back.

Dutch metal A colored metallic foil used in gilding as a cheaper substitute for gold or silver leaf.

E

earth pigments Pigments obtained from earths rich in minerals such as iron oxides – see pp.222–5.

eaves The projecting edges of a roof.

ebonized Wood stained black to resemble ebony.

egg tempera A paint consisting of powder pigments, linseed oil, water, and egg yolk.

egg-and-dart A decorative molding made up of alternating egg and arrow (or V) shapes.

églomisé French term for gold-backed glass.

Elements Earth, wind, fire, and water, derived from Greco-Roman mythology and science.

Empire style A style originating in France in the 1790s. An Imperial Roman variant of the *Neoclassical style, patronized by Napoleon Bonaparte and accommodating Egyptian, *Etruscan, and military motifs.

en-suite A French term used to describe the practice of duplicating or closely matching fabrics or colors used on different surfaces or objects in the same room.

entablature The top part of an *Order, made up of an *architrave, a *frieze, and a *cornice.

Etruscan style A style inspired by that of the ancient civilization of Etruria, centered in Tuscany and Umbria, Italy, from the 7th to the 2nd century B.C. Characterized by red, black, and white color schemes, and by motifs such as lions, birds, *sphinxes, and *griffins.

F

fanlight A window above a door, usually semicircular, with *glazing bars radiating out like a fan. Also known as a transom window.

fauteuil French term for an armchair with upholstered back, arms, and seat, introduced in the mid-18th century.

faux marbre French for fake marble. A technique for simulating the appearance of marble with paints.

Federal style The predominant style of architecture and decoration in North America from the mid-1770s to the early 19th century. Based on *Adam style, it also included French *Neoclassical and, later, *Empire style.

ferrule A metal band, ring, or cap.

festoon In Greco-Roman ornament, a garland, often containing *aegricanes. From the *Renaissance it often included *rosettes, lion masks, and *putti.

field The section of a wall that extends down from the *cornice or *frieze to the top of the *dado.

fielded panel A raised panel.

figuring Patterns formed by the grain of a wood.

finial A carved or molded ornament on top of a spire, gable, post, or chairback, or the ends of curtain rods.

fire dogs Iron supports, are also known as andirons, used to support the ends of burning logs in a hearth.

flock Wallpaper with a raised, textured pattern of fine particles of wool or other fibers.

floorcloth A floor covering made from canvas stiffened with *linseed oil, then painted or stenciled with patterns.

fluting Shallow, concave, parallel grooves running vertically on a column or other surface.

foil A lobe or leaf-shaped curve inside an arch or circle.

fresco A method of painting, dating to ancient Egypt, in which *tempera paints are applied to wet plaster.

fretwork Pierced geometrical ornament of intersecting straight, repeated, vertical and horizontal lines.

frieze The section of wall from the ceiling or *cornice to the top of the *field. Often embellished with motifs.

fugitive Describes pigments and dyes that, when exposed to light, air, or water, tend to fade, streak, or mottle.

G

gable Part of a wall directly under the end of a pitched roof, cut to a triangular shape by the sides of the roof.

gambrel roof A type of roof with a lower part constructed at a steeper pitch than the upper part.

gesso A fine plaster mainly used as a thin covering on wooden moldings prior to gilding.

girandole A convex mirror.

glazing bars The bars, usually wooden, that secure panes of glass in a window frame.

Gobelin A tapestry factory established in Paris in 1622.

Gothic The prevalent style of architecture in the *Middle Ages, characterized by pointed arches, ribbed *vaults, *arcading, galleries, *tracery, and naturalistic imagery.

Gothic revival A 19th-century revival of Gothic architectural forms and ornamentation (see above).

Gothick A rather romanticized, late-18th century English version of the *Gothic revival.

Greco-Roman Collective term for the architecture, ornament, and decoration of Ancient Greece and Rome.

Greek Revival A *Neoclassical style inspired by the architecture of Ancient Greece.

griffin Mythical beast with the head, wings, and claws of an eagle and the body of a lion.

grisaille A monochromatic *trompe l'oeil technique.

grotesques Motifs from ancient Roman wall paintings including animals, *medallions, and *scrolling foliage.

grotto In nature a cave, but also an ornamental man-made cave with decorative, shell-encrusted walls.

Gustavian style A Swedish *Neoclassical style of the late 18th century – see pp.106–113.

gypsum Hydrated calcium sulfate used to make plaster.

H

hacienda Spanish term for an estate or ranch.

half-tester A bed with an overhead canopy extending from a pair of headposts halfway down the bed.

hand-blocked Paper or fabric printed using wooden blocks bearing all or part of a pattern, dipped in pigment and pressed down on the surface to be printed.

hardwood Lumber from deciduous trees whose slow growth produces a compact hard wood, such as oak.

hematite An iron ore used as a red pigment.

Heraldic imagery Used in the *Middle Ages to denote status and lineage in feudal society. Typical motifs were *cyphers, *coats-of-arms, shields, lions, and *griffins.

hieroglyphs Characters used in picture writing.

High Victorian A style popular in England c.1850–80, characterized by richly colored, densely furnished interiors, elaborate fabric furnishing, and many artifacts.

highboy A high chest-of-drawers.

hue Term used to describe a color, and therefore to distinguish one color from another.

Huguenots Alternative name for French Protestants.

husks A stylized budlike motif, also known as bellflower.

I

Imari A type of Japanese porcelain made in the 17th and 18th centuries. It featured dense *brocadelike patterns and a palette of blue, iron-red, and gilding.

indigo A blue pigment obtained from both *woad and an Asian plant, but also made synthetically from 1896.

ingrain carpet An inexpensive type of pileless carpet.

Ionic One of the Classical *Orders characterized by fluted columns and prominent *volutes on the *capitals.

iroko An African hardwood.

Italianate Mid-19th-century architecture based on that of rural northern Italy and Italian Renaissance palaces using overhanging eaves, round-headed windows, corner *quoins, arcaded porches, and balustraded balconies.

J

Jacobethan A collective term used to describe 16th-century Elizabethan and early 17th-century Jacobean architecture and decoration.

jambs The vertical sides of a doorway, an arch, or a fireplace – sometimes in the form of *pilasters.

japonaiserie A European interpretation of Japanese art, featuring dragons, birds, and flowering plants as motifs.

K

kelim A flat-weave rug woven in the Middle East.

key stone The central stone in the curve of an arch.

L

lampblack A black pigment made from burning carbon.

lancet A thin pointed window in *Gothic architecture.

lap pool A moatlike pool around the perimeter or part of the perimeter of a house or courtyard.

lapis lazuli An ultramarine colored stone; also a deep blue color (sometimes veined with gold).

latex A modern water-based paint made from pigmented emulsion of plant resins.

lead glaze Thick, transparent ceramic glaze containing lead oxide that can be colored with metallic oxides.

limewash A traditional paint consisting of water, slaked lime, and pigment used to paint plaster and stone walls.

limonite An iron ore that yields a brown pigment.

Lincrusta A durable waterproof wall and ceiling paper invented in 1877, and made from *linseed oil, gum, resins, and wood pulp spread over canvas. Embellished with relief in imitation of wooden or plaster moldings.

linoleum A durable floorcloth patented in 1860 and made from *linseed oil, *resin, and gum on a canvas backing. Often colored and patterned in imitation of other materials such as marble and wood.

linseed oil A translucent oil extracted from flax and used to make oil-based paints.

lintel A supporting beam across the top of an opening, such as a doorway, a window, or a hearth.

lusters Candlesticks ornamented with cut-glass pendants.

M

madder A red dye from a plant of the *Rubia* genus.

magnetite An iron ore that yields a black pigment.

malachite A green copper-carbonate pigment.

medallions Circular or oval devices applied to plasterwork, silver, porcelain, and textiles.

Mesoamerican The area of central America covering northern Mexico and Panama.

mezzotint A form of copperplate engraving.

Middle Ages Period from the fall of the Roman Empire in the 5th century A.D. to the Renaissance.

milk paint Inexpensive and durable paint made from milk, earth, or vegetable pigments and a little lime.

Modern style see pp.130–5

moiré A watered or wavelike appearance on ribbed fabric, usually heavy silk, or wallpaper.

moreen A woven ribbed cloth with a *moiré*-like pattern.

mosaic A pattern made of small pieces of colored ceramics, stone, or glass.

mull A *muslin-like cotton fabric.

muslin An inexpensive, coarse, lightweight cotton fabric.

N

Neoclassical style see pp.60–3

newel The post at the end of a staircase. On winding staircases it is the central post around which the stairs curve that supports the narrow side of the steps.

O

ogee arch A pointed arch formed by two reversed curves that are slightly S-shaped in profile.

onyx A colorful variegated marble.

open-string A staircase in which the side or sides of the treads and *risers (the steps) are exposed.

Orders The architectural components that constitute the basis of Classical Greek and Roman architecture. Each Order consists of a *column usually rising from a pedestal or plinth, topped by a *capital and supporting an *entablature. The styles of Order include Doric, Ionic, Corinthian, Tuscan, and Composite.

oriel window A bay window on an upper floor.

ornamentistes French term for artists and designers who specialize in engraved designs of ornament.

overmantel The decorative treatment of the wall above a fireplace, often incorporating a painting or mirror.

P

paisley Pattern of stylized pine cones of Oriental origin, but developed in Paisley, Scotland, in the 19th century.

Palladian motif Alternative term for *Venetian window.

Palladianism see Early Georgian style, pp.30–35

papyrus A plant from Ancient Egypt, whose stems were cut and pressed to form a paperlike writing material.

parlor A family living room.

parquet A floorcovering of wooden blocks laid in a decorative geometric pattern.

pastoral imagery Romanticized images and motifs derived from rural life and the countryside popular in the 18th century.

patera A circular or oval motif, frequently decorated with *acanthus leaves or *fluting.

patina Attractive and desirable surface sheen resulting from years of handling, polish, and dirt.

pediment A low-pitched (triangular-shaped) *gable across the top of a *portico, door, window, or fireplace.

Pegasus The winged horse of Classical mythology.

piano nobile The principal floor of a large house.

pickling Treating wood with a lime solution to protect against insect infestation. Gives a grayish-white cast.

pier glass A tall mirror hung between windows.

pilaster A flat, usually rectangular column, often decorated with * reeding or *fluting.

pinnacle A turret or turretlike ornament, often employed in *Gothic architecture.

plywood A board made of thin layers of wood pressed and glued together.

pocket door A door that slides into a recess in a wall.

portico A roofed porch, usually supported on columns.

portière A curtain hung over a doorway.

Post-Modernism see pp.136–57

primary colors Red, yellow, and blue.

Prussian blue A blue pigment – a precipitation of an iron and cyanide solution – with a greenish cast first made in Berlin (the capital of Prussia) in 1704.

Pueblos A native North American tribe.

putti Depictions of sweet-faced, chubby infants, the attendants of Eros and Cupid, the Greek and Roman gods of love.

pyrites An iron disulfide that yields yellow pigment.

Q

quoins The dressed stones at the corners of a building, sometimes simulated in wood.

R

rafter An inclined beam used to support a roof.

reeded A surface decorated with parallel strips of narrow convex moldings divided by grooves.

Regency style see pp.78–81

Renaissance The revival of the Classical Greco-Roman vocabulary of architecture and ornament, which flourished in Europe from the 14th to the 16th centuries.

riser The vertical surface of a step.

Rococo style see pp.54–9

Romanesque The style of architecture prevalent in Europe in the 11th and 12th centuries, inspired by Classical Rome, but including other forms and motifs.

rosette Circular, stylized floral motif.

roundel A circular ornament.

row house One house in a row all attached by their side walls.

runner A narrow rug or carpet, primarily employed in a hall or on a staircase.

S

sash A window that slides up and down in vertical grooves controlled by counterbalanced weights.

saturated A term used to describe a color with a high *chromatic intensity.

sconce A bracketed candlestick (can be wall-mounted).

scrolling foliage A form of ornament consisting of scrolling, curving plant forms, such as *acanthus plants.

secondary color A color made by mixing together two *primary colors.

secrétaire French term for a writing desk.

sepia A fine brown pigment either derived from cuttle fish or produced synthetically.

serpentine A sinuous, snakelike profile.

shade A darker version of a color made by mixing it with black.

Shaker style see pp.202–7

Shingle style A late 19th-century style of architecture in the U.S., which combined wooden siding and *gambrel roofs with dormers and oriel windows.

siderite An iron ore that yields a brown pigment.

slips The fascia installed between the opening of a hearth and the *jambs of a mantelpiece.

socle Either a plain plinth that forms the foundation of a wall, or a plinth for a statue, column, or vase.

sphinx A monster, of ancient Egyptian origin, with the head of a woman and the body of a lioness.

Stick style Type of wood-frame house built in the U.S. during the late 19th century. Partly derived from Swiss chalets and characterized by wide surrounding verandas.

stretcher A cross-bar or horizontal member used to brace the legs of a piece of furniture.

stucco A fine cement or plaster applied to the surface of walls and *moldings.

swags Loops of drapery; also pendant garlands of flowers, fruits, vegetables, leaves, or shells.

T

tapestry-woven Fabrics woven with a bobbin and comb, rather than on a loom.

tempera see *egg tempera.

terracotta A form of unglazed earthenware made from clay and sand; a brownish-red color.

terrazzo A polished finish for floors and walls consisting of marble or stone chips set in mortar.

tertiary color Made by mixing *primary and *secondary colors.

ticking A twill-weave cotton fabric with evenly spaced stripes. Mainly used to cover mattresses and pillows.

tint A lighter version of a color made by mixing it with white.

toile de Jouy The printed cottons, or "toiles," made at the Jouy factory in France. Patterned with narrative pictures in monochrome; the most common subjects are *chinoiserie* and romantic scenes of rural life.

Toltec An ancient *Mesoamerican civilization.

tongue and groove Joint made between a groove in one piece of wood and a tongue in another.

tracery Riblike bars used to ornament the upper part of a window in *Gothic architecture.

transfer printing Method of printing on ceramics by transferring a design from an inked copper plate.

Tree of Life A design originated in Ancient Persian and Indian art, with a tree at its center symbolizing the "life force." Popular in England in the 17th century.

trelliswork A form of woodwork and a decorative motif styled on the traditional crisscross support for plants.

trompe l'oeil French for "trick of the eye." A decorative technique in which paints or dyes are applied to a flat surface to create the appearance of three-dimensional scenes or objects.

turpentine A viscous resin mainly derived from conifer trees and used as a solvent for oil paints.

Tuscan One of the *Orders of architecture.

V

valance A piece of fabric, generally stiffened with a backing, set above a window to conceal the curtain pole and the top of curtains.

vaulted Arched, as in an arch-shaped roof or ceiling.

vegetable dyes see pp.226–9

Venetian window A window with an arched-top center section flanked by two narrower rectangular sections.

veranda A roofed but otherwise open gallery, porch, or balcony supported by posts.

verdigris Derived from the French for "green of Greece," a bluish-green pigment obtained by scraping off the patina from copper that has been exposed to vinegar fumes.

vermilion A strong red pigment made, prior to *c*.1785, from cinnabar (a naturally occurring form of mercuric sulfide); thereafter it was also made synthetically by heating mercury and sulfur.

Veronese green An emeraldlike, chrome-based green named after the Italian painter, Paolo Veronese.

Victorian style see pp.116–129

volute A spiral, scrolling form, probably based on the shape of a ram's horn.

W

wattle-and-daub A method of wall construction consisting of branches or thin laths (wattles) roughly plastered over with mud or clay (daub). Often used as a filling between the members of wood-framed houses.

weld A yellow dye derived from mignonette, a plant of the *Reseda* genus also known as "dyer's rocket."

Wilton carpet A *Brussels-weave carpet with a looped pile that is cut to give it a soft, velvety finish. First produced in the mid-18th century in Wilton, England; thereafter in the rest of Europe and the U.S.

woad A blue vegetable dye – see pp.226–9.

woodgraining A decorative technique in which paints and glazes are applied to a softwood to simulate the color, figuring, and grain of a more expensive hardwood.

Z

ziggurat A pyramid-shaped temple-tower with a number of stories, each successively smaller than the one below.

Directory

Paint Suppliers

Brats Ltd
281 Kings Road
London
SW3 5EW
tel: 020 7351 7674
fax: 020 7349 8644
email: info@brats.co.uk
www.brats.co.uk

**Casa Paint supplied by
Relics of Witney**
35 Bridge Street
Witney, Oxon
OX8 6DA
tel/fax: 01993 704611
email: sales@relics.demon.co.uk
www.relics.demon.co.uk

**Colonial Williamsburg
Foundation**
P.O. Box 1776
Williamsburg
Virginia, 23187 USA
tel: 757 229 1000
www.history.org

Colourman Paints
Coton Clanford
Stafford, Staffs
ST18 9PB
tel: 01785 282799
fax: 01785 282292

**Crown Paints supplied by
Akzo Nobel Decorative Coatings
Limited**
P.O. Box 37, Crown House
Hollins Road
Darwen, Lancs
BB3 OBG
tel: 01254 704951
www.akzo.nobel.com

Cy-Près
14 Bells Close
Brigstock
Kettering, Northants
NN14 3JG
tel/fax: 01536 373431

Dulux
Wexham Road
Slough, Berks SL2 5DS.
tel: 01753 550555
www.dulux.co.uk

Farrow & Ball
Uddens Trading Estate
Wimborne
Dorset BH21 7NL
tel: 01202 876141
fax: 01202 873793
email: farrow-ball@farrow-ball.com
www.farrow-ball.com

Fired Earth plc
Twyford Mill
Oxford Road, Adderbury
Oxon OX17 3HP
tel: 01295 812088
fax: 01295 810832
email: enquiries@firedearth.com
www.firedearth.com

Ace Hardware Paint Division
21901 South Central Avenue
Matteson
Illinois 60443
USA
tel: 708 720 0600, fax: 708 720 1347

**Jane Churchill paint supplied by
Farrow & Ball**
(as above)

John Oliver Ltd
33 Pembridge Road
London W11 3HG
tel: 020 7221 6466/020 7727 3735
fax: 020 7727 5555

Liz Induni
11 Park Road
Swanage
Dorset BH19 2AA
tel: 01929 423776
email: induni@tesco.net

Marston & Langinger
192 Ebury Street
London SW1W 8UP
tel: 020 7824 8818
fax: 020 7824 8757
email: sales@marston-and-langinger.com
www.marston-and-langinger.com

**Natural Color System supplied by
J.W. Bollom & Co. Ltd**
P.O. Box 78, Croydon Road
Beckenham, Kent BR3 4BL
tel: 020 8658 2299
fax: 020 8658 8672
www.bollom.com

**The Old Fashioned
Milk Paint Co. Inc.,**
436 Main Street
P.O. Box 222, Groton
MA 01450–0222
USA
tel: (978) 448 6336
fax: (978) 448 2754
email: sales@milkpaint.com
www.milkpaint.com

**Old Village Paints supplied by
Lawrence T. Bridgeman Ltd**
No. 1 Church Road
Roberttown
Liversedge
West Yorkshire WF15 7LS
tel: 01924 413813
fax: 01924 413801

Paint Library
5 Elystan Street
London SW3 3NT
tel: 020 7823 7755
fax: 020 7823 7766
email: davidoliver@paintlibrary.co.uk

Paint Magic Ltd
48 Golborne Road
London W10 5PR
tel: 020 8960 9960
fax: 020 8960 9655
email: paintmagic.ltd@virgin.net
www.paint-magic.com

**Ralph Lauren Paint
supplied by Janovic**
30–35 Thomson Avenue
Long Island City
NY 11101
USA
tel: 718 786 4444
Out of state 1 800 772 4381
fax: (718) 361 7288
email: info@janovic.com
www.janovic.com

Rose of Jericho
Westhill Barn
Evershot, Dorchester
Dorset DT2 0LD
tel: 01935 83676/83662
fax: 01935 83017
email: info@rose-of-jericho.demon.co.uk
www.rose-of-jericho.demon.co.uk

Sanderson
100 Acres, Sanderson Road
Uxbridge
Middlesex UB8 1DH
tel: 01895 238244
fax: 01895 231450
email: cvc@a-sanderson.co.uk
www.sanderson-uk.com

Shaker Ltd
72–3 Marylebone High Street
London, WIM 3AR
tel: 020 7935 9461
fax: 020 7935 4157
email: shaker@shaker.co.uk
www.shaker.co.uk

Places to Visit

France

Bleus de Pastel de Lectoure
Ancienne Tannerie
Pont de Pile
32700 Lectoure
email: bleupastel@aol.com
www.bleu-de-lectoure.com

Château du Champ de Bataille
27110 Le Neubourg

Italy

Family Bianchi Bandinelli
Villa di Geggiano
Via Geggiano, 1
53010 Pianella
Siena
email: villadigeggiano@tin.it

Morocco

Ministero del Gusto
Design Gallery
22 Derb Azouz
El Mouassine
Marrakesh-Medina 40000
email: mingusto@cybernet.net.ma

Mexico

Malinalco Golf Club
Carretera Joquicingo-Malinalco s/n
San Sebastián Amola
Malinalco, Estado de México, 52440
email: golfmalinalco@mail.dsinet.com.mx

Spain

Patrimonio Nacional
Palacio Real de Aranjuez
Calle Bailén, S/N
28071 Madrid
email: gab.cultural@
patrimonionacional.es
www.patrimonionacional.es

Sweden

Julita
Sveriges Lantbruksmuseum
Julita 64025
www.nordm.se/slott/julita.html

UK

Osterley Park
Jersey Road
Isleworth, Middlesex
TW7 4RB
email: tosgen@smtp.ntrust.org.uk
www.nationaltrust.org.uk

USA

The Austin House
www.wadsworthatheneum.org

Bernd Goeckler Antiques Inc.
30 East 10th Street
New York
NY 10003
email: BGoeckler@aol.com
www.BGoecklerAntiques.com

Boscobel Restoration, Inc.
1601 Route 9D
Garrison
NY 10516
New York
email: info@boscobel.org
www.boscobel.org

Bowen House, Roseland Cottage
On the common
556 Route 169
Woodstock
CT 06281–2344
www.spnea.org

Colonial Williamsburg Foundation
Williamsburg
23185 Virginia
www.history.org

Hancock Shaker Village
Routes 20 and 41
P.O. Box 927
Pittsfield
MA 01202
email: info@hancockshakervillage.org
www.hancockshakervillage.org

The Mark Twain House
351 Farmington Avenue
Hartford
CT 06105
email: desk@hartnet.org
www.hartnet.org/twain

The Morris–Jumel Mansion
65 Jumel Terrace
New York
NY 10032–5360

Old Merchant's House Museum
29 East 4th Street
New York
NY 10003–7003
email: nyc1832@merchantshouse.com
www.merchantshouse.com

The Wadsworth Atheneum
600 Main Street
Hartford
CT 06103–2911
www.wadsworthatheneum.org

Webb-Deane-Stevens Museum
211 Main Street
Wethersfield
CT 06248
email: wdsmuseum@freewwweb.com
www.webb-deane-stevens.org

Places to Stay

Italy

Hotel Torre di Bellosguardo
Via Roti Michelozzi n. 2
50124 Florence
email: torredibellosguardo@dada.it
http://members.aol.com/PuterBugzz
/tbellos.html

Sarah and Guigi Maria Sesti
Castello di Argiano
53020 S. Angelo in Colle
Montalcino, Siena

Mexico

Las Alamandas
Quemaro, Costalegre
Jalisco 48980
email: alamanda@zonavirtual.com.mx
www.las-alamandas.com

Hacienda de San Antonio
San Antonio
Comala, Colima 28450
email: lahacienda@compuserve.com
www.haciendasanantonio.com

Morocco

Dâr Tamsna
Route de Fès
La Palmeraie, Marrakesh-Medina
Postal address:
B.P. 262 Marrakesh-Medina
Marrakesh
email: dartamsna@cybernet.net.ma

Dâr Zellij
102 Rue Dar El Bacha
Marrakesh-Medina 40000
email: rak.medina@cybernet.net.ma
www.marrakech-medina.com

La Maison Arabe
1 Derb Assehbe
Bab Doukkala,
Marrakesh

Villa Maroc
10 Rue Abdellah Ben Yassine
Essaouira 44000
email: hotel@villa-maroc.com
www.villa-maroc.com

UK

Lena Proudlock
Drews House
Leighterton
Gloucestershire
GL8 8UN
email: lenaproudlock@aol.com

Architects & Designers

France

Jacques Garcia (Designer)
212 Rue de Rivoli
75001 Paris

Italy

Piero Castellini Baldissera
(Designer)
Via Morozzo della Rocca 5
Milan 2010023

Mexico

Javier Sordo Madaleno (Architect)
Paseo de la Reforma 2076A
Lomas de Chapueltepec
11000 Mexico City
email: sma@data.net.mx

Manuel Mestre (Architect)
Parque Via Reforma 2009
Lomas de Chapueltepec
Mexico City 11000
email: mmestre@mail.internet.com.mx

de Yturbe Architects
de Yturbe Golf Design
Sierra Mojada 626–2
Lomas de Barrilaco
Mexico City 11010
email: deyturbe@infosel.net.mx
www.deyturbe.com

UK

Timothy Everest (Tailor/Designer)
Studio/Workshop
32 Elder Street
Spitalfields
London E1 6BT
email: timothyeverest@dial.pipex.com

Christophe Gollut (Designer)
116 Fulham Road
London SW3 6HU
email: Nfbruce@cs.com

Index

Acknowledgments

The Publishers thank the following photographers and agencies for their kind permission to reproduce the photographs in this book:

10 AKG, London; 11 James Morris/Axiom; 12 National Archaeological Museum, Greece/Bridgeman Art Library; 13 Erich Lessing/AKG, London; 14 Château de Pierrefonds, France/Peter Willi/Bridgeman Art Library; 15 Angelo Hornak (Courtesy of Leeds Castle, Kent); 16 Richard Bryant/Arcaid; 17 E.T. Archive; 18 English Heritage Photographic Library; 19 Colonial Williamsburg Foundation; 20 Erich Lessing/AKG, London; 21 English Heritage Photographic Library; 22 Richard Bryant/Arcaid; 23 Angelo Hornak (Courtesy of the Royal Pavilion, Brighton); 25 Erich Lessing/AKG, London; 38–43 Colonial Williamsburg Foundation; 52–3 Colonial Williamsburg Foundation; 54 **above** Erich Lessing/AKG, London; 56 **left** AKG, London; 58 **above centre** Schloss Schönbrunn, Austria/Bridgeman Art Library; 58 **below left** Erich Lessing/AKG, London; 59 **above** Joseph Martin/AKG, London; 59 **centre** Erich Lessing/AKG, London; 78 **above** Simon Upton/Interior Archive; 78 **below right** Fritz von der Schulenburg/Interior Archive; 79 **left** and 80 **below right** V&A Picture Library; 81 **above** Simon Upton/Interior Archive; 131 Paul Raftery/Arcaid © FLC/ADAGP, Paris & DACS, London, 2000; 172–5 Hacienda de San Antonio, S.A. de C.V. – **Photographs:** Armando Mendoza; 186–7 Hacienda de San Antonio, S.A. de C.V. – **Photographs:** Armando Mendoza; 202 **above** and **below left** Hancock Shaker Village, Pittsfield, MA.– **Photograph:** M. Fredericks; 202 **below right** Paul Rocheleau; 203 **left** Paul Rocheleau; 203 **right** Hancock Shaker Village, Pittsfield, MA. – **Photograph:** Paul Rocheleau; 204 Herbert Ypma/Interior Archive; 205 Herbert Ypma/Interior Archive; 206 **above left** and **centre** Paul Rocheleau; 206 **above right** Hancock Shaker Village, Pittsfield, MA. – **Photograph:** Paul Rocheleau; 206 **below left** Hancock Shaker Village, Pittsfiled, MA. – **Photograph:** M. Fredericks; 206 **below right** Herbert Ypma/Interior Archive; 207 **above left** Paul Rocheleau; 207 **above right** Herbert Ypma/Interior Archive; 207 **centre left** Hancock Shaker Village, Pittsfield, MA. – **Photograph:** Paul Rocheleau; 207 **centre right** Paul Rocheleau; 207 **below** Shaker Ltd

Every effort has been made to trace the copyright holders and we apologize in advance for any unintentional omission and would be pleased to insert the appropriate acknowledgment in any subsequent editions.

The Publishers and I would like to thank the following for their kind permission to photograph their homes, businesses and places of work and for all their help with this project.

FRANCE
Andrew Allfree; Lillian Williams; Jacques Garcia; Roberto Bergero and Philippe Safavi; Amélie Dillemann; Denise and Henri Lambert; Gloria and Eric Stewart; Yves and Raphaelle de Montvert

ITALY
Piero Castellini Baldissera; Amerigo Franchetti at Hotel Torre di Bellosguardo; Andrea Boscu Bianchi Bandinelli at Villa di Geggiano; Sarah and Guigi Maria Sesti

MEXICO
Javier Sordo Madaleno; José de Yturbe and Enrique Martin-Moreno; Manuel Mestre; Isabel Goldsmith

MOROCCO
Villa Maroc; La Maison Arabe; Dâr Zellij; Alessandra Lippini and Fabrizio Bizzarri; Meryanne and Gary Loum-Martin

SCANDINAVIA
Patricia Lindstrom; Lars Sjöberg

SPAIN
María del Prado Dégano Alejo at the Patrimonio Nacional, Madrid

UK
Hew Stevenson and Leslie Geddes-Brown; Keren Manley at Osterley Park; John and Annie Nethercott; Lena Proudlock; Timothy Everest; the late Michael Gillingham; Paula Pryke and Peter Romanuik; Mary and Etienne Millner Christophe Gollut

US
Jane Nylander and Catherine Mageau at the Bowen House, Roseland Cottage (SPNEA); Carol Stoliar at Old Merchant's House Museum; Joanna Pessa at The Morris–Jumel Mansion; Fred Hughes; Charles T. Lyle and Karen Dunn at Boscobel Restoration, Inc.; Donna Baron at Webb-Deane-Stevens Museum; Stephen Rice at The Mark Twain House, Hartford, CT; Alexander and Megan Julian; Eric and Nanette Brill; Bernd Goeckler; Fayal Greene

I would like to thank Tim Clinch for his wonderful location photography, and Graham Vickers for contributing to the text. I would also like to thank everyone in the team at Marshall Editions for bringing their skills and enthusiasm to the book: Jess Walton for location and picture research; Anne-Marie Bulat for initial design concept; Dave Goodman for art direction, and Nigel Soper and Flora Awolaja for design; Ellen Dupont for overseeing the project, and Liz Stubbs for running it so efficiently; Christine Davis and Charles Phillips for skillfully editing the text and Victoria Cookson for her editorial assistance; Hilary Bird for indexing; Nikki Ingram for production control; and Maggi McCormick for Americanizing the text.